“With her typical care and cl[illegible] accessible exploration not only of the important idea of genres but also of how they can be nested inside one another. The introduction and case studies model for us a thoughtful and fruitful reading of Scripture.”

—**Jonathan T. Pennington**, Southern Seminary

“The best approach to the interpretation of any biblical text begins with genre identification. In this book, Jeannine Brown polishes our ‘genre-sensitive lens’ to help us detect changes that reveal genres embedded within other forms. This hermeneutical practice sheds light on layers of meaning within the world of the text that have thus far gone unnoticed. Brown is both clear and convincing.”

—**David B. Capes**, Lanier Theological Library

“A proper understanding of ancient genres is fundamental to biblical interpretation. But since each scriptural text consists of a variety of literary forms, the task of interpreters extends beyond merely identifying the characteristics of a single type of literature; readers must also account for the use of one genre in another. It is surprising, therefore, that this topic has received so little attention within modern scholarship. This book fills the lacuna perfectly, however. By carefully delineating the function and significance of embedded genres, Jeannine K. Brown has supplied readers of the New Testament with a valuable resource, one that brings fresh interpretive perspective to familiar texts.”

—**Travis B. Williams**, Tusculum University

“New Testament scholar Jeannine Brown draws from a deep well of experience and expertise in biblical interpretation. In *Embedded Genres in the New Testament* she offers a fresh look at how the microgenres within biblical books relate to their macrogenre and why that matters for more-faithful interpretation. Every interpreter of the Bible, whether a professional or a serious student, will benefit from Brown's latest work."

—**Karen H. Jobes**, Wheaton College (emerita)

"At its best, biblical exegesis is a journey of discovery, in which the attentive reader sees and hears the text afresh. Brown's nuanced study takes her readers on just such a journey, both modeling fine-grained historical and literary attention to the dynamics of embedded genres and giving her readers the tools to do the same. This book is a boon to all serious teachers and students of the New Testament."

—**Susan Eastman**, Duke Divinity School (emerita)

"Brown has distinguished herself as an expert on biblical hermeneutics and exegesis, and here she illuminates 'embedded genres,' micro-literary pieces within a larger text. Brown offers a convincing case that readers benefit greatly from keen awareness of where these embedded units occur, how they deserve special attention, and how they affect the whole. She fills a gap left by textbooks that often miss this important topic."

—**Nijay K. Gupta**, Northern Seminary

"Sometimes I think good interpretation of the Bible is about slowing down—taking notice of, puzzling over, sitting with scriptural texts. Sometimes I think it's about better readerly habits—listening (really listening!), asking good questions, exploring. Centering our attention on embedded literary forms in the Bible, on how they shape and are shaped by the books in which they appear, Jeannine Brown cultivates good habits by urging us to slow down and listen up. Her work with texts from Philippians, Matthew, and 1 Peter is stimulating on its own terms, and even more so as she addresses larger interpretive possibilities and invites us to do the same."

—**Joel B. Green**, Fuller Theological Seminary

# EMBEDDED GENRES IN THE NEW TESTAMENT

## Acadia Studies in Bible and Theology

*H. Daniel Zacharias, General Editor*

The last several decades have witnessed dramatic developments in biblical and theological study. Full-time academics can scarcely keep up with fresh discoveries, ongoing archaeological work, new exegetical proposals, experiments in methods and hermeneutics, the rise of majority world theology, and innovative theological proposals and syntheses. For students and nonspecialists, these developments can be confusing and daunting. What has been needed is a series of succinct studies that assess these issues and present their findings in a way that students, pastors, laity, and nonspecialists will find accessible and rewarding. Acadia Studies in Bible and Theology, sponsored by Acadia Divinity College in Wolfville, Nova Scotia, and in conjunction with the college's Hayward Lectureship, constitutes such a series.

The Hayward Lectureship has brought to Acadia many distinguished scholars of Bible and theology, such as Sir Robin Barbour, James D. G. Dunn, C. Stephen Evans, Edith Humphrey, Leander Keck, Helmut Koester, Richard Longenecker, Martin Marty, Jaroslav Pelikan, John Webster, Randy Woodley, and N. T. Wright. Initiated by Lee M. McDonald and Craig A. Evans, the Acadia Studies in Bible and Theology series continues to reflect this rich heritage and foundation.

These studies are designed to guide readers through the ever more complicated maze of critical, interpretative, and theological discussion taking place today. But these studies are not introductory in nature; nor are they mere surveys. Authored by leading authorities in the field, the Acadia Studies in Bible and Theology series offers critical assessments of major issues that the church faces in the twenty-first century. Readers will gain the requisite orientation and fresh understanding of the important issues that will enable them to take part meaningfully in discussion and debate.

# EMBEDDED GENRES IN THE NEW TESTAMENT

## Understanding Their Impact for Interpretation

JEANNINE K. BROWN

Baker Academic
a division of Baker Publishing Group
Grand Rapids, Michigan

Published by Baker Academic
a division of Baker Publishing Group
Grand Rapids, Michigan
www.bakeracademic.com

Printed in the United States of America



Library of Congress Cataloging-in-Publication Data
Names: Brown, Jeannine K., 1961– author.
Title: Embedded genres in the New Testament : understanding their impact for interpretation / Jeannine K. Brown.
Description: Grand Rapids, Michigan : Baker Academic, a division of Baker Publishing Group, [2024] | Series: Acadia studies in Bible and theology | Includes bibliographical references and index.
Identifiers: LCCN 2023040910 | ISBN 9781540967619 (paperback) | ISBN 9781540967725 (casebound) | ISBN 9781493445936 (ebook) | ISBN 9781493445943 (pdf)
Subjects: LCSH: Bible. New Testament—Criticism, Form. | Bible. New Testament—Criticism, interpretation, etc. | Literary form.
Classification: LCC BS2377 .B76 2024 | DDC 225.6/6—dc23/eng/20231122
LC record available at https://lccn.loc.gov/2023040910

Unless otherwise noted, Scripture quotations are the author's own translation.



Cover art of Echternach Bible from Chronicle, Alamy Stock Photo
Cover design by Paula Gibson

Baker Publishing Group publications use paper produced from sustainable forestry practices and post-consumer waste whenever possible.

24 25 26 27 28 29 30 7 6 5 4 3 2 1

# CONTENTS

# PREFACE

It was my privilege and pleasure to deliver the Hayward Lectures in October 2022 at Acadia Divinity College. I was grateful that I was able to be at Acadia in person after a two-year hiatus, during which the lectures were held virtually due to the global pandemic. Acadia faculty and staff warmly welcomed me and provided such a hospitable space for me to join in their vibrant community. I want to thank Matthew Walsh (Old Testament specialist), who chauffeured me to Wolfville from the Halifax airport and portended the genuine care and welcome of the entire Acadia community. A special thank you to Danny Zacharias (New Testament specialist and director of the Hayward Lectures) for the invitation to give these lectures; for wonderful conversations about the New Testament, Matthew, and indigenous interpretation throughout the days I was at Acadia; and for his able editing of this volume.

When I was asked to give the Hayward Lectures and given my choice of topics, my mind turned fairly quickly to hermeneutical and literary facets of New Testament interpretation. My prior work in the area of hermeneutics and in genre particularly,[1] along with my recent commentary work in Philippians,[2] prompted my

1. Brown, *Scripture as Communication*, now in its second edition; and an earlier essay on literary and rhetorical contributions to genre (Brown, "Genre Criticism").

2. Brown, *Philippians*.

lecture topic, "Hymns, Riddles, and *Haustafeln*: The Hermeneutical Significance of Embedded Genres in the New Testament." As I was completing my work in Philippians for the Tyndale commentary series, I was convinced I had more to learn and explore regarding Philippians 2:6–11, what I had come to refer to in that commentary as the "Christ poem." I was intrigued by the ways scholars had tussled over whether this section of Philippians was a hymn or poem, or whether it continued the letter's prose, albeit in an elevated form. The entire topic of embedded genres began to be a point of fascination. My already established interest in the Petrine household code became a second area of study for these lectures.[3] Finally, my career-long focus on Matthew became a venue for fresh exploration as I embarked on an analysis of riddles in this Gospel, drawing on the excellent work of Tom Thatcher.[4] After giving the lectures, the development of this monograph allowed for time and space for more focused study on the hermeneutical issue of embedded genres, and I dove into this topic with great interest and with a renewed appreciation for contemporary rhetorical study of genres, which has given the most attention to this specific literary and rhetorical category.

In addition to Danny Zacharias and the Acadia Divinity College community, I also thank Baker Academic for their (as always) exceptional editorial guidance. I am also grateful to two research assistants at Bethel Seminary, Narah Larson and Heather Brannock, who read and commented on the lectures and on the chapters (respectively). I was also helped along by a gathering of the Twin Cities New Testament Symposium in January 2023, which graciously allowed me to present my ideas from chapter 1 and gave me excellent input for strengthening that work.

3. Brown, "Silent Wives" and "Just a Busybody?"

4. I had begun to recognize more riddles in Matthew and had reflected these occurrences in my commentaries on that Gospel (e.g., Brown and Roberts, *Matthew*), but I have been helped for this book in extraordinary ways by Tom Thatcher's insights in *Jesus the Riddler*.

As I was writing the introduction for my lectures and was searching out an ideal (nonbiblical) example of embedded genre, I landed on the various letters from one character to another in Jane Austen's *Pride and Prejudice*. At the time I didn't realize how fruitful this example would be (rhetorical and literary theorists explicitly discuss this use of embedded genre). I was drawn to Austen out of a long-standing admiration for her work and a shared joy of reading her novels within our family. Early in our acquaintance, my husband and I bonded over our mutual appreciation of this author. And we chose to name our daughters with her beloved characters in mind. It is to my younger daughter, Elizabeth Austen Brown Cook, an admirer of Austen and a teacher of literature to middle schoolers, that I dedicate this book.

# ABBREVIATIONS

| | |
|---|---|
| BDAG | Danker, Frederick W., Walter Bauer, William F. Arndt, and F. Wilbur Gingrich. *Greek-English Lexicon of the New Testament and Other Early Christian Literature*. 3rd ed. Chicago: University of Chicago Press, 2000 |
| CEB | Common English Bible |
| CSB | Christian Standard Bible |
| ET | English translation |
| KJV | King James Version |
| LCL | Loeb Classical Library |
| LXX | Septuagint |
| MT | Masoretic Text |
| NIV | New International Version (2011) |
| NKJV | New King James Version |
| NLT | New Living Translation |
| NRSVue | New Revised Standard Version, updated edition |
| *TDNT* | *Theological Dictionary of the New Testament*. Edited by G. Kittel and G. Friedrich. Translated by G. W. Bromiley. 10 vols. Grand Rapids: Eerdmans, 1964–76 |
| *TLNT* | *Theological Lexicon of the New Testament*. C. Spicq. Translated and edited by J. D. Ernest. 3 vols. Peabody, MA: Hendrickson, 1994 |

ONE

# How Do Embedded Genres Matter?

In the interpretation of any writing, including the books of the Bible, identifying genre is a key factor for understanding what a particular author is communicating. We won't understand what we are reading if we don't know *what it is* we are reading.[1] Fortunately, we evaluate and adapt to what we read—the genre of a work—pretty seamlessly, especially as we engage materials in our own culture and setting. When I sit down at a restaurant, I know how to read and understand a menu. When I pick up Jane Austen's *Pride and Prejudice*, I know how to go about comprehending it because I have encountered other novels of its kind and even other novels by the same author.

## Obstacles to Genre Awareness

When we come to interpret the Bible, however, there are at least a couple of factors that can complicate the ease with which we

1. J. R. Martin and David Rose tightly connect genre to meaning, describing genres as "configurations of meaning" (*Genre Relations*, 231).

normally enter any particular piece of writing from our own time and place. First, some biblical genres may simply be unfamiliar to us. Today, we have nothing quite like the Jewish genre of apocalyptic, which is the primary genre of the book of Revelation. This means we'll be hard pressed to intuitively understand Revelation at every turn. And even readers who have experience with a genre that occurs in the Bible—take poetry, for example—could be unfamiliar with the particulars of Hebrew or Jewish poetry, which is not identical to English or Western poetry.[2] For contemporary readers of ancient texts, it can be important to ask, "How are we to know when we should leave our 'intuitive' expectations at the door and when those expectations may actually be helpful for interpretation?"[3]

Second, genre is, in much of our experience, a hidden variable in interpretation. As Mikhail Bakhtin suggests about the production side of genre, "Our repertoire of oral (and written) speech genres is rich. We use them confidently and skillfully *in practice*, and it is quite possible for us not even to suspect their existence *in theory*."[4] And on the reception side of things, Sune Auken notes, "We are able to perform highly complex interpretive moves through genres without realizing that we are interpreting—much less that we are interpreting through genre."[5] Our very familiarity and comfort level with genre as a fundamental facet of communication can mask the numerous interpretive moves we intuitively make to

2. This fits with Sune Auken's suggestion that "one of the hardest things in dealing with genres from a different culture—be it foreign, historical, or both—is to understand that which is implied in any given genre use" ("Contemporary Genre Studies," 54).

3. Brown, "Genre Criticism," 112.

4. Bakhtin, *Speech Genres*, 78.

5. Auken, "Contemporary Genre Studies," 54. Hindy Najman offers two ways of conceiving of genre, one tied to textual production (assuming the author's awareness of genre norms) and one tied to textual reception (with the reader providing the classification of texts in genres) ("Idea of Biblical Genre," 309). She then suggests the image of a constellation for understanding how a "non-generic class of texts" hangs together by the arrangement (the constellation) of certain features. "Constellations depend for their legibility on our interests as readers. Still, they are objectively there" (316).

understand any particular utterance or piece of communication. Bakhtin helpfully describes genre assessments that happen fairly intuitively: "When hearing others' speech, we guess its genre from the very first words; we predict a certain length (that is, the approximate length of the speech whole) and a certain compositional structure; we foresee the end; that is, from the very beginning we have a sense of the speech whole, which is only later differentiated during the speech process."[6] All this is done with minimal conscious awareness, especially in genres that we feel at home with as part of our own culture and context.[7]

Another complicating factor is particularly applicable to any of us who read the Bible *as Scripture*. Often by virtue of our commitment to the Bible as divinely inspired, we can unintentionally *flatten* its various parts toward a single voice—a single form. And we might even wonder, *If it is all Scripture, is it important to notice or highlight differences among the various parts of the Bible, genre included?* Glenn Paauw notes that even the way the English Bible has traditionally been formatted and laid out, with two columns to a page, has *functionally* obscured genre distinctions. "In a two-column Bible everything appears relentlessly the same. Israel's ancient song lyrics, pithy proverbs, lengthy narratives, first-century letters—one wouldn't know about any of this from the looks of it."[8] According to Paauw, something as seemingly innocuous as formatting has tended to obscure the distinct genres we encounter within the Bible.

## Embedded Genres and Hermeneutics

Now let's add a point of further complexity and the one that occupies this book: *genres embedded in other genres*. An embedded

6. Bakhtin, *Speech Genres*, 79.
7. Bailey, "Genre Analysis," 140.
8. Paauw, *Saving the Bible*, 44.

genre adds to the hermeneutical complexity of genre analysis, since book-level genres themselves can contain or include quite an array of short literary forms.[9] Bakhtin refers to these as "primary (simple) genres" that often are embedded or woven into more complex, "secondary (complex) genres."[10] In contemporary genre studies, scholars have used the language of "hybridity" (a general term for all kinds of genre mixing) and of "genre embedding," which refers to the use of one genre within another genre.[11] Anne Mäntynen and Susanna Shore define "genre embedding" as occurring when "an entire text is incorporated as a clearly distinguishable part of another text."[12] These authors go on to note, "Embedding is often seen as a conventionalized and integral feature of many genres."[13] As an example, we can consider how letters are embedded in Austen's novel *Pride and Prejudice*. In fact, the epistolary genre is embedded all across this nineteenth-century novel, with more than forty letters being used by Austen to advance the plot.

We can see this phenomenon quite readily in the Gospels of the New Testament. As an example, we can identify within Mark, whose "macrogenre"[14] fits the category of Greco-Roman biography (*bios*), quite a number of shorter embedded genres. Broadly speaking, these fall within two groupings: narrative forms (like miracle stories, pronouncement stories, conflict stories) and say-

9. Brown, "Genre Criticism," 137.

10. Bakhtin, *Speech Genres*, 62. Bakhtin notes that it is often the case that "simple genres" (e.g., embedded ones) are oral in origin and form. This is the case for the embedded genres discussed below in chapters 2 (Phil. 2:6–11, if it is a preexisting hymn) and 3 (riddles in Matthew).

11. Mäntynen and Shore, "Hybridity," 738, 745. They describe genre "hybridizing" as the issue of "how (parts of) a text representing one genre can be incorporated into another text representing another genre or mix of genres" (742).

12. Mäntynen and Shore, "Hybridity," 745. Auken's definition is similar: "a genre that is included within the framework of another genre" (Auken, "Genres inside Genres," 164).

13. Mäntynen and Shore, "Hybridity," 746.

14. Also termed "complex genre" (see Mäntynen and Shore, "Hybridity," 751).

ings forms (like parable, proverb, riddle, blessing).[15] As Eve-Marie Becker notes, "Mark has combined different types and strands of traditions like 'sayings' and narrative traditions" to compose his macrogenre.[16] She goes on to write, "On a *narrative and on an interpretive* level Mark . . . creates a comprehensive literary concept, i.e., a gospel-writing in which the diverse sequences of Jesus' ministry are connected."[17] The macrogenre of Gospel incorporates as a matter of course quite a number of microgenres.

All to say, the practice of genre embedding is commonplace, both in contemporary texts and in ancient ones like those in the Bible. As Auken notes, "Almost everywhere, genre goes, embedded genres follow, and our competency in understanding and using genre is closely intertwined with our mastery of embedded genres."[18] Nevertheless, if genre is often a hidden, or at least muted, variable in interpretive practice, this seems to go doubly for embedded genres. If the interpretive moves we make based on genre tend to happen "under the radar," how much more might this be the case about the embedded genres we encounter along the way?

Scholarly discussions of genre have not yet taken full account of the hermeneutical significance of embedded genres. This is true within biblical studies as well as in literary and rhetorical studies. In the latter orbit—in contemporary rhetorical discussions of genre—"only rarely do scholars move into the embedded genres that make up an utterance."[19] In biblical studies, extended analysis of embedded genres is a noticeable lacuna. While traditional form

15. Form criticism, a subdiscipline of biblical studies, has focused on these "microgenres" and sought to identify them as well as describe their uses as oral forms prior to being incorporated in the Gospels.

16. Becker, "Reception of 'Mark,'" 24.

17. Becker, "Reception of 'Mark,'" 24.

18. Auken, "Genres inside Genres," 164.

19. Auken, "Contemporary Genre Studies," 61. Elsewhere, Auken notes that the discussion of embedded genres "plays a limited role in existing genre research" ("Genres inside Genres," 165).

criticism was keenly attentive to what Bakhtin has called "primary forms,"[20] this focus did not typically extend to the sophisticated interplay between secondary genres (entire books) and the primary forms that populate them, since the common form-critical assumption was that no great nuance or authorial effect existed on the macrolevel.[21]

Recent primers on biblical hermeneutics, including my own, provide only limited space to the phenomenon.[22] William Klein, Craig Blomberg, and Robert Hubbard give more attention to embedded genres than most. In addition to cataloging common embedded genres in both Old and New Testaments, they also delineate principles for analyzing embedded genres.[23] James Bailey and Lyle Vander Broek offer what might be the fullest discussion of embedded genres in their *Literary Forms in the New Testament*. They address key forms (what I am calling "embedded genres") that occur within the various larger genres of the New Testament—for example, epistles and narratives. In the Pauline Letters, they explore the diatribe, topoi, vice and virtue lists, the household code, and poetry or hymn, among others. In narrative, they discuss aphorism, parable, various kinds of stories (e.g., miracle, pronouncement, commissioning), and genealogy, to name some.[24] In each chapter they also address the value for interpretation gained by identifying and giving attention to the patterns or tendencies of these embedded forms. One of the interpretive

20. Bakhtin, *Speech Genres*, 62.

21. Becker observes the "literary underevaluation of Mark" in form criticism generally ("Reception of 'Mark,'" 25n50). In contrast, she asserts that "the Markan Gospel is much more than a contingent collection of traditions" (25). See also Brown, "Genre Criticism," 119.

22. Brown, *Scripture as Communication*, 145, 153, 160 (for what I refer to as "subgenres"). In *Invitation to Biblical Interpretation*, Andreas Köstenberger and Richard Patterson identify a variety of embedded genres (e.g., 276–78, 424–26, 473–76).

23. Klein, Blomberg, and Hubbard, *Biblical Interpretation*, 437 ("principles for interpretation"), 433–37 (common Old Testament embedded genres), 523–32, 551–55 (common New Testament embedded forms).

24. For a comprehensive list, see Bailey, "Genre Analysis," 150–51.

gains they highlight is an awareness of how any particular form is modified and adapted for the New Testament author's specific purposes.[25]

Taking our cues from this conversation, however limited, biblical interpreters should consider more closely the use of embedded genres within biblical books. Indeed, if genre identification is crucial to interpretation, then attention to embedded genres is equally essential. This is an especially important task, given what I have suggested is a tendency to flatten biblical texts into an unbroken whole. To recognize and take account of embedded genres, interpreters will need to be keenly alert to shifts in genre within any particular book of the Bible. As J. R. Martin and David Rose suggest for embedded genres, "As a general rule, the better our genre analysis, the easier it will be to recognize genres as we come across them."[26] Having our genre antenna raised, not just at the beginning of biblical books but also within them, is an important hermeneutical skill. We can begin by looking out for changes in structure, pacing, language use, register, and perspective, which may signal a midstream shift in genre.

Just as we can trust that on the whole-book level "works themselves guide the reader toward their generic affinities,"[27] we can assume that authors provide adequate signals for the embedded genres populating their works. As Wayne Booth affirms, "Though actual readers will make of their works whatever their generic expectations enable them to make, works themselves work very hard, as we might say, to put up 'dead end' signs and directional arrows that actually work."[28] Embedded genres provide "directional arrows" that point toward their genre affinities. For instance, while

25. See, for example, Bailey and Vander Broek, *Literary Forms*, 69–71 (household codes), 81–82 (poetry), and 103–4 (aphorisms). For an interpretive example of a narrative text embedded in a letter (1 Cor. 11:23b–25), see also Bailey, "Genre Analysis," 159–60.

26. Martin and Rose, *Genre Relations*, 235.

27. Brown, "Genre Criticism," 136.

28. Booth, *Rhetoric of Fiction*, 435.

Luke at times signals the inclusion of a parable with the language of *parabolē* (e.g., Luke 12:16), he also uses a common feature of a parable, the introduction “a certain person” (*anthrōpos tis*), without explicit reference to *parabolē* (14:16). Other indications of parable as an embedded genre include its storied shape, a key conflict in the plot (Luke 14:18–21), and a closing aphorism (14:24).

Once a potential embedded genre is identified, we can turn to the tendencies of that genre to confirm its presence and assist in its interpretation.[29] We can draw an example from the Letter to the Romans to explore the interpretation of embedded genres. At the conclusion of Romans 9–11, a major segment of the letter and one that is devoted to Paul’s consideration of God’s ongoing covenant loyalty to Israel in spite of the seeming rejection of Jesus as the Messiah by many from Israel, Paul turns to poetic praise (or doxology). We can observe a fairly clear shift from a prose explanation of God’s wide and merciful plan for both Israel and gentiles (11:28–32) to shorter poetic lines, effusive language, and parallel ideas and repetitions in 11:33–36.[30] Quite a number of contemporary translations helpfully set off this section of text as poetry.[31]

> **33** Oh, the depth of the riches of the wisdom and
> knowledge of God!
> How unsearchable his judgments,
> and his paths beyond tracing out!
> **34** “Who has known the mind of the Lord?
> Or who has been his counselor?”
> **35** “Who has ever given to God,
> that God should repay them?”

29. E. D. Hirsch suggests that genre typifications provide “conceptual wedges” into a text (*Validity in Interpretation*, 116).

30. Paul incorporates a citation from Isaiah (40:13) in Rom. 11:34, and possibly an allusion to Job 41:11 at Rom. 11:35, both themselves poetic texts.

31. Some of these keep 11:33 as prose, and a few also show 11:36 as a prose line (i.e., they set off 11:34–35 or 11:34–36 as poetry).

> 36 For from him and through him and for him are all things.
> To him be the glory forever! Amen. (Rom. 11:33–36 NIV)

This formatting helps the reader to see the embedded genre of poetry and interpret it according to its poetic parameters. Interpreting an embedded genre begins by doing just that—shifting our genre expectations from the macrogenre of the whole book to the specific embedded genre (the microgenre), now identified. Different genres require different reading strategies, and recognizing a shift between genres allows us to bring a genre-sensitive lens to the embedded form. Once we carefully interpret the embedded genre according to its inherent characteristics and tendencies, we can then explore how the microgenre contributes to its context. As Klein, Blomberg, and Hubbard guide, "The goal of interpretation [of an embedded genre] is to find what that component contributes to the message of the whole."[32]

In the case of the Romans doxology, the movement from prose to poetry illuminates Paul's desire to praise God for the wisdom of the unfolding of divine mercy to both Jew and gentile. Additionally, the poetic turn signals that the ideas Paul has been engaging—the unexpected twists and turns of the story of God's commitment both to Israel and to the nations—ultimately elude human comprehension. What Paul writes in 11:33–36 (about the inscrutability of God's ways) and how he writes it (in poetry) combine to communicate this truth.

An interpretive insight drawn from rhetorical discussions of embedded genres is that the interpretive process needs to move in both directions, since, as much as the embedded genre impacts the macrogenre or text, the macrogenre also has interpretive effect on the embedded genre. This is called "recontextualization" by some genre theorists,[33] and it involves the recognition that the

32. Klein, Blomberg, and Hubbard, *Biblical Interpretation*, 437.
33. Mäntynen and Shore, "Hybridity," 745.

embedded genre does not remain unaffected in its use within the wider macrogenre. Each genre mutually impacts the other. As Auken describes recontextualization,

> The reason why genres embed other genres in the first place, or why complex genres are built from simpler, is that the embedded genre carries its own character into the new context, adding meaning to it. By consequence, interpreting a complex genre necessitates a coherent understanding of the many simpler genres that constitute it. Thus, *there is a dialectic relationship between the two levels*. The embedded genres are transformed by their new generic context, but features are carried over from the original genre specifically to influence this new context. Thus, a genre will be defined by the genres it embeds, and will in turn define those genres.[34]

In hermeneutical reflection on embedded genres in New Testament studies, the directional influence typically has moved from the embedded genre to the macrogenre. In other words, the interpretive focus has been on how the embedded form impacts the larger context. And this is certainly a proper hermeneutical emphasis since authors draw on an embedded form for specific rhetorical purposes for their overarching work. Nevertheless, it can also be helpful to consider how the book-level genre might impact the shorter, embedded form being used. Both questions can be hermeneutically generative if there truly is "a dialectic relationship" between the embedded and book-level genres.

## Analysis of an Embedded Genre: Letters in *Pride and Prejudice*

To get a feel for this dialectic relationship, or bidirectional influence, between a micro- and macrogenre, let's return to Jane

34. Auken, "Genres inside Genres," 166 (italics added).

Austen's *Pride and Prejudice*. As already noted, quite a number of letters written by one character to another make their way into Austen's narrative.[35] And these letters often signal key narrative and even climactic moments in the plot. There's Caroline Bingley's letter to Jane announcing that their whole party, including her brother, has left the country to return to London—dashing Jane's hopes and disrupting her budding romance with Mr. Bingley (chap. 21). An important pair of letters come at a key moment in the story line: Jane's two letters to the away-from-home Elizabeth—received together one fateful morning—revealing the catastrophic news of their sister Lydia's reckless elopement with Mr. Wickham (chap. 46).

Undoubtedly, the most memorable letter in *Pride and Prejudice* is Mr. Darcy's letter to Elizabeth after her rejection of his proposal of marriage (chap. 35). Barbara Heller refers to this letter as "the thematic heart of the novel."[36] Given that Austen has made the reader privy to Elizabeth's thoughts but seldom Darcy's in her narrative, this letter is a treasure trove containing Mr. Darcy's point of view and experiences. The embedded genre of letter allows Austen to reveal more of this character's "first person" perspective without changing the direction of her own way of being the third-person narrator (i.e., a limited versus an omniscient narrator). As Jodi Devine suggests, "With Darcy's letter . . . , the readers see more sides to his character and insights into his thinking beyond what the narrator tells us."[37]

35. Indeed, *Pride and Prejudice* may have been originally conceived as an epistolary novel (*First Impressions*), although this is a matter of some debate. Austen's *Sense and Sensibility* was first written as an epistolary novel.

36. Heller, introduction to *Pride and Prejudice*, by Jane Austen, 7. Heller further suggests that Darcy's "letter is a proxy for the man, affording [Elizabeth] time and space to contemplate him" (7).

37. Devine, "Epistolary Revelations," 3. She also notes, "With the use of letters in her novels, Austen gains the advantage of an epistolary novelist by having the letters 'speak' for the characters' consciousness" (16).

I suggest that readers of *Pride and Prejudice* will intuitively change direction (i.e., change their reading strategy) when they arrive at one of these letters (clearly marked out as such) and will read them as the first-person voice of the character who has written it. They will intuitively move a step closer to that character, especially in the letters where the personal thoughts and experiences of the character are laid bare. And they will learn to look for important plot twists and turns that arise with these letters. (Readers will learn that these are not places for skimming.)

And if we follow the insight from rhetorical genre studies that embedded genres are also impacted by their *embeddedness*, we can note that the letters of *Pride and Prejudice* take on specific qualities from their existence in the genre of novel. In fact, the novel is what gives them their sender and recipient; the characters in the novel provide the "reality" for each letter in its existence as a letter. Auken frames it in this way: "A letter in a novel has no actual existence and does not fulfill the material, formal, and communicative requirements for a letter. However, within the framework of the diegesis it reacquires its normal characteristics; it has a writer and a reader, is a non-fictional document written by the writer for the purpose of perusal by the reader, and has a clear—albeit fictional—materiality; the letter-in-the-novel is perceived [within the story] as real."[38]

In *Pride and Prejudice*, we can explore a specific example of the impact on a letter from its narrative context (i.e., its embeddedness in the genre of novel) in the pair of letters from Jane to Elizabeth that are received at the same time (because, in addressing the first letter, "Jane had written the direction remarkably ill" [chap. 46]). The first letter has a more innocuous tone than the second, with Jane expressing her initial understanding that Lydia has eloped with Mr. Wickham to Scotland—an "imprudent . . . match on both sides" but not a matter of great alarm. Yet the arrival of the

38. Auken, "Genres inside Genres," 166.

second letter at the same time as the first creates greater anticipation and narrative tension since the reader is being prepared for a fuller account and does not have to wait for a second post (just as Elizabeth experiences no delay between the two letters). The inopportune news of the first letter at least suggests that the second may contain worse news, creating a sense of foreboding as Elizabeth opens it: "Without allowing herself time for consideration, and scarcely knowing what she felt, Elizabeth on finishing [the first] letter, instantly seized the other, and opening it with the utmost impatience, read as follows" (chap. 46).

Therefore, there is good narrative reason for Austen having the first letter go astray. It heightens the narrative tension and paves the way for the devastating news that Lydia has not eloped but has gone off with Mr. Wickham, who seems to have no plans to marry her. And it allows Elizabeth (and the reader) to encounter the two-part news report from home in quick succession (a one-two punch, as it were). This, in turn, sets the stage for the untimely arrival of Mr. Darcy and Elizabeth's disclosure of the disturbing news to him—a disclosure that likely would not have occurred if she had received the letters at two different times.

## Analysis of an Embedded Genre: Matthew's Genealogy

As we turn to consider interpreting embedded genres in the New Testament and doing so by paying attention to bidirectional influence, let's take as an example Matthew's genealogy (Matt. 1:2–16). Kasper Bro Larsen poses the key question for bidirectional interpretation: "How does the primary/simple genre contribute to and function in the text as a whole, and how does the whole color the primary/simple genre and its traditional ideologies and functions?"[39]

39. Larsen, "John as Genre Mosaic," 17.

The genealogy follows directly upon Matthew's opening title (1:1): "The account of the origin of Jesus the Messiah, son of David, son of Abraham."[40] Other than this title, Matthew chooses to begin his *bios* or biography of Jesus (the macrogenre of this Gospel) with a genealogy. The embedded genre—the genealogy—contributes to this biography of Jesus in a number of ways, but one in particular highlights the bidirectional influence of embedded genre and macrogenre in Matthew 1. As genealogies are intended to do, this genealogy appears to be used to affirm the legitimacy of Jesus' lineage and particularly to demonstrate Jesus to be the culmination of David's kingly line.[41] Yet Matthew's conclusion to the genealogy problematizes the inclusion of Jesus in the line of Joseph:

> Jacob was the father of Joseph, who was the husband of Mary.
> And Jesus, who is called the Messiah, was conceived by Mary. (1:16)

It is Mary alone, not Joseph, "from whom Jesus was begotten [*gennaō*]" (a wooden rendering of 1:16b), with the relative pronoun (*hēs*) being a singular feminine and so excluding Joseph. This creates a "conundrum" for the genealogy's assumed function,[42] shifting the significance of this genealogy from its typical use of legitimizing Jesus to questioning the attribution of Joseph's line to him. By the end of Matthew 1, however, the reader can apply the genealogy to Jesus and so the genealogy can fulfill its

40. The evangelist's dual use of *genesis* ("origin") at 1:1 and at 1:18 seems to indicate that the opening title covers the whole of chapter 1 (or, possibly, all of 1:2–4:16) and not just the genealogy of 1:2–16. Translations of Matthew are my own, from Brown and Roberts, *Matthew*.

41. The emphasis on David comes in 1:6, where David is the only ancestor called "king," as well as in the shaping of the genealogy in segments of fourteen (1:17)—a gematria for David's name.

42. Brown and Roberts, *Matthew*, 29.

typical function. The reader can do so because Matthew answers the "conundrum" of 1:16 in his narration of Jesus' conception and birth in 1:18–25. There, Matthew affirms that Joseph names Jesus, adopting him as his own and so bringing him into his family line.[43] The biographical narrative of Matthew—the macrogenre—impacts the embedded form by providing the solution to the problem raised in the genealogy's conclusion. The genealogy impacts the narrative by offering, albeit in an unusual and circuitous way, its legitimizing function for Jesus' family line.[44] Embedded genre and macrogenre thus interact to provide a hermeneutical dialectic.

## Conclusion

My goal in this book is to capture a deeper sensitivity to embedded genres in the New Testament by exploring three test cases, one each from Philippians, Matthew, and 1 Peter. I hope to explore how interpreters might move nimbly and thoughtfully between the book-level genres of these three writings to embedded genres within them. In each case, it will be crucial to shift our "reading strategy" as we move from the overarching genre to the differing form embedded within it.[45]

In chapter 2, I take on a contested (so a potential) embedded genre: poetry within the letter of Philippians (2:6–11). *Does Paul break into song in this passage?* In chapter 3, we'll explore what I suspect is an underidentified (though not especially contested) embedded genre in Matthew's Gospel, the riddle, and its use by

43. The significance of naming and of Jesus' name in these verses connects to the cultural feature of fathers naming their children to suggest that Matthew shows Joseph adopting Jesus into his family and so into his family line (Brown and Roberts, *Matthew*, 29).

44. This example illustrates Auken's proposal: "These simpler [embedded] genres lose part of their original character when they are used as building blocks, but they also add meaning to the overarching, secondary genre" ("Contemporary Genre Studies," 66).

45. Longman, *Literary Approaches*, 83.

Jesus. The question we'll engage is whether Jesus is portrayed as a *riddler* in Matthew. In chapter 4, I'll address a genre form that is well recognized and sits prominently at the center of the letter of 1 Peter. There I'll ask, *Why put a household code at the center of 1 Peter?*[46] In each case, the goal will be (1) to explore the features of the embedded genre that identify it as an example of that form, (2) to analyze how the embedded genre contributes to the larger macrogenre, and (3) to reflect on how the author's incorporation of the microgenre into the larger whole might, however subtly, impact that embedded form.

46. A form that Luther referred to as the *Haustafel* and that still is referred to as such in the scholarly literature.

TWO

# Does Paul Break into Song in Philippians 2?

## *The Christ Poem in the Letter to the Philippians*

On a trip to London when our girls were young, my husband, Tim, purchased same-day tickets for *Les Misérables*. Neither of our daughters had seen the musical or even listened to the music. As we sat in the fourth row of the theater, Fantine sang "I Dreamed a Dream." The girls were spellbound. Our oldest, Kate, then twelve years old, turned to me as Fantine finished the last note and whispered in solemn voice, "That's my favorite song."

Such is the power of music—of song, of poetry. After marinating in the Christ hymn of Philippians 2:6–11 during the writing of a commentary on that letter, I felt something of that awe, that impact that Kate felt. And I have come to say of the Philippian Christ hymn, "That's my favorite song."

But does Paul really break into song in Philippians 2? The question of the genre and form of Philippians 2:6–11 has been and continues to be hotly debated. A hundred years ago, scholars routinely viewed it as an early Christian hymn, predating Philippians, that Paul used and adapted. This "Christ hymn" was often reconstructed by scholars from what we have in Philippians 2:6–11. Recent scholarship, however, has tended to discount the form-critical arguments for a preexisting "Christ hymn." They have, rightly I suggest, emphasized how the purported "hymn" functions in Philippians 2. Whether borrowed or Paul's own creation, what remains in the text is thoroughly Pauline. As Michael Gorman nicely sums it up, "Whether or not Paul wrote it . . . , he clearly owned it."[1] In the process of reaffirming the text in context, however, some have discounted its poetic genre as part of the larger argument against viewing the passage as a preexisting hymn.[2]

Michael Martin and Bryan Nash have recently revived the hymn argument for Philippians 2 by examining what the Greek and Latin rhetoricians have to say about *hymnos* as a genre. What they find is that "the topical form of the hymn—and not its poetic form—is what secures its identification as a hymn," since a *hymnos* can be written in either poetry or prose.[3] Their work suggests that we should be able to determine if Philippians 2:6–11 is a poem without assuming that this settles the question of whether it is a hymn.[4]

1. Gorman, "Cruciform Way," 68.

2. In other words, the form-critical hymnic identification may have contributed to later hesitance to call this text poetic after the early Christian hymn theory lost favor (akin to throwing out the baby with the bathwater). To strengthen arguments against identifying this passage as a preexisting hymn, there may have been a tendency to minimize its poetic character more generally.

3. Martin and Nash, "Subversive *Hymnos*," 136. According to their analysis, the four "consistently attested generic markers" of *hymnos* that emerge from a study of the rhetorical handbooks are species of rhetoric, subject, length, and topic lists (96–97).

4. Martin and Nash, "Subversive *Hymnos*," 136. On the other hand, a determination of this passage as a hymn does not settle the question of whether it is poetic.

So, to adjust slightly the earlier question, we could ask, Does Paul break into poetry here? Or, does Paul simply continue his epistolary prose as he moves from 2:1–5 to 2:6–11, even if it is an "exalted prose"—a view suggested by Gordon Fee in an influential article of thirty years ago: "Philippians 2:5–11: Hymn or Exalted Pauline Prose?"[5] The question of the genre of Philippians 2:6–11 is the focus of this chapter, and I will argue that this text is indeed formally poetry—"the Christ poem," as I refer to it.[6] Based on this genre identification, we will also explore the significance of recognizing its poetic form for understanding its meaning in context.

## Philippians 2:6–11 as Poetry

Although the King James Version did not (and does not) indicate the presence of poetry in its translation, the majority of modern translations show poetry with shorter line lengths and other visual cues, such as placing lines in stanzas.[7] Of those translations that visualize poetry on the page, the majority display Philippians 2:6–11 in poetic form. Yet scholars of Philippians debate—and debate vigorously—whether these six verses of Philippians are full-blown poetry or something more like elevated prose.

To set out plainly and quite starkly the scholarly genre debate, we can compare the two views side by side. The comparison can be most starkly seen in two quotations from G. Walter Hansen

5. Adele Berlin speaks to the somewhat fluid distinction between poetry and prose: "Elevated style is largely the product of two elements: terseness and parallelism. Where the two occur to a high degree we have what would be called . . . poetry; where they are largely (but never entirely) lacking, we have . . . what we call prose." (*Dynamics of Biblical Parallelism*, 5).

6. Fee (and others who follow his lead) readily acknowledges that Phil. 2:6–8 (and even 2:9–11) has poetic qualities (*Philippians*, 192–93), although Fee suggests that 2:9–11 "lacks both . . . poetry and balanced clauses" (196). Fee's primary interest appears to be discounting that 2:6–11 is a (pre-Pauline) "hymn" ("Philippians 2:5–11").

7. See, for example, how modern translations format the psalms.

and Gordon Fee, respectively, on the question of the genre of Philippians 2:6–11.

> The rhythmic cadence, the parallel patterns and lines, the framing of independent verbs with participles, and the bipartite structure of the entire hymn with the downward movement of humiliation perfectly counterbalanced by the upward movement of exaltation are all poetic elements that *set this text apart from the usual style of Paul.*[8]

> This passage lacks the rhythm and parallelism that one might expect of material that is to be sung. . . . In Paul's Greek, as exalted as it is, the sentences follow one another in perfectly orderly prose—*all quite in Pauline style.*[9]

With this kind of divide, with such a seeming impasse, how can we go about identifying whether this passage is poetry?[10] What does poetry look like in the first century? This first question immediately raises the prior question of the origin or kind of poetry in view. What does poetry look like in the Greek world of Paul's time, since Philippians is written in Greek? Or should we be looking at Jewish antecedents for the elevated cadences of Philippians 2 since Paul demonstrates that he is thoroughly familiar with his own Scriptures?

For the most part, scholars have highlighted the resemblance of New Testament poetry with its Jewish antecedents. The poetry that New Testament authors incorporate into their writings (whether borrowed or their own composition) routinely follows

8. Hansen, *Philippians*, 128 (italics added).

9. Fee, "Philippians 2:5–11," 31 (italics added).

10. Moisés Silva's comment resonates with Hansen's: "Even the label 'elevated prose' does not do justice to the rhythm, parallelisms, lexical links, and other features that characterize these verses" (*Philippians*, 93). Others who identify Phil. 2:6–11 as poetry include Bockmuehl, *Philippians*, 116; Gaebelein, "New Testament Poetry," 248; Fowl, *Story of Christ*, 24.

poetic patterns from the Jewish Scriptures.[11] As Floyd Filson observes, "The New Testament is [written] in Greek, but it contains only the briefest echoes of Greek poetry or poetry patterns. If, then, there is original poetry in the New Testament, it must be found by relating the material to Semitic poetic patterns."[12] What we have in Philippians 2, I suggest, is "a poetry composed in Greek but following a Hebrew poetics."[13]

If this assessment is accurate, we can begin by identifying some of the key facets of Jewish (i.e., Hebrew-based) poetry and see if and how these appear in Philippians 2. We begin with the observation by Old Testament scholar F. W. Dobbs-Allsopp that "so much of what goes on in biblical poems does so at the level of the line."[14] While prose, at least in an epistle, is often carried along by an author's extended argument (often using complex structures and embedded clauses), in poetry meaning is conveyed through the interrelationships between and among poetic lines. We can think of these interrelationships on two levels: the macrolevel and the microlevel.

### *Poetic Lines: Macrolevel Structures*

We begin by analyzing Philippians 2 for the "higher poetic units" of strophes and stanzas featured in Jewish poetry.[15] On

11. We can observe these poetic patterns within the Septuagint, even though early LXX copies do not always show poetic lines in their formatting in the intertexts relevant to Phil. 2:6–11 (e.g., in the Prophets [Isaiah] or in Gen. 1:27).

12. Filson, "Poetry," 126.

13. This is Matthew Whitlock's description of Lukan poetry ("New Testament Poetry," 90). Stephen Fowl suggests that the use of Jewish poetic conventions in Greek texts is not at all unusual, and he provides the examples of Sir. 51 and Jdt. 16 (*Story of Christ*, 23). See also Hansen, *Philippians*, 132.

14. Dobbs-Allsopp, *On Biblical Poetry*, 9. This begs the question of how to determine a line of poetry. While any number of scholars argue that a lack of meter makes it virtually impossible to determine the line divisions of Phil. 2:6–11, which itself is viewed as an argument against its poetic form, it is important to remember that Hebrew poetry has little in the way of meter. "Jewish poetry—including that written or translated in the Greek language—entirely lacks Greek metre and is characterized instead by poetic figures and the form and rhythm deriving from these" (Martin and Nash, "Subversive *Hymnos*," 136).

15. Zogbo and Wendland, *Hebrew Poetry*, 62 (see pp. 62–67).

this level, poetry can include "large-scale envelope structures, such as inclusios . . . and chiasms."[16] There are a number of "envelope structures" on the macrolevel of Philippians 2:6–11, each of which points to identifying this passage as poetry. The first set of structural clues involves the repetition of forms and of key words in what I contend to be the first two stanzas of the poem (vv. 6–7b and vv. 7c–8).[17]

As a first instance of repetition,[18] we can compare the first line of each of these proposed stanzas and notice that each is a formal mirror to the other (v. 6a and v. 7c). In Greek, both lines consist of the same opening preposition (*en*) + a dative noun + a genitive noun + a final participle (which expresses verbal action).

| Verse | *en* + Dative Noun | Genitive Noun | Participle |
|---|---|---|---|
| 6a | "in the form"<br>*en morphē* | "of God"<br>*theou* | "being"<br>*hyparchōn* |
| 7c | "in the likeness"<br>*en homoiōmati* | "of humans"<br>*anthrōpōn* | "being made"<br>*genomenos* |

These formal correspondences in the first line of each stanza are augmented by careful repetition of key words across both stanzas.

16. Dobbs-Allsopp, *On Biblical Poetry*, 191–92 (in reference to the psalms specifically).

17. I follow Joachim Jeremias in his formulation of two stanzas for Phil. 2:6–8 ("Zu Phil ii 7," 186–87); see also Cohick, *Philippians*, 117. For the alternative view that 2:6–8 comprises three stanzas, see Silva, *Philippians*, 93–94 (although he also speaks to the strengths of the two-stanza configuration [99]); Bockmuehl, *Philippians*, 125. Scholars who argue that this passage is poetic divide 2:6–8 into either two or three stanzas. "For some, the lack of consensus on versification argues against identifying it as a fully developed poem. Yet the inability of contemporary, non-native Greek speakers, working on a text that was not initially laid out in poetic (or any kind of) lines, to reconstruct its poetic particulars would be unremarkable. And such exacting reconstruction is not a prerequisite for identifying significant poetic features in 2:6–11, as well as drawing on its poetic genre to guide interpretive work on the text" (Brown, *Philippians*, 109). Similarly, Gerald Hawthorne and Ralph Martin "refuse to accept as valid the proposition that a correct understanding of the hymn depends on an agreed versification of the hymn" (*Philippians*, 102); see also Bockmuehl, *Philippians*, 126.

18. As Edward Hirsch contends, "One of the deep fundamentals of poetry is the recurrence of sounds, syllables, words, phrases, lines, and stanzas" (*Poet's Glossary*, 518).

6a Who, though being in the **form** [*morphē*] of God [*theos*],
6b did not consider equality with God [*theos*] as something to be exploited;
7a rather, he emptied himself
7b by taking the **form** [*morphē*] of a slave.
7c **Being made** [*genomenos*] in the likeness of human beings [*anthrōpoi*][19]
7d and being found in appearance as a particular human being [*anthrōpos*],
8a he humbled himself
8b by **becoming** [*genomenos*] obedient to death,
8c all the way to death on a cross.[20]

The word *morphē* ("form") provides an *inclusio* or bookend around the first stanza and accents the potent contrast between Christ's preexistent reality "in the form of God" (6a) and the result of his emptying—"taking the form of a slave" (7b). In the second stanza, the Greek participle *genomenos* provides the *inclusio* for the stanza by showing the movement from Christ "becoming" (or "being made") human to Christ "becoming" obedient, even though it involved the most ignoble death the first-century world knew—crucifixion.

The interrelationship between these first two stanzas is further emphasized by the repetition of the two realities of Christ's identity: *theos* ("God") is repeated in the poem's first two lines to accent Christ being in "the form of God" and sharing "equality with God" (6a and 6b). The same kind of structural repetition occurs in the first two lines of the second stanza (7c and 7d).

19. This line is included in verse 8 in many English versions (e.g., KJV, ESV, NIV). In my versification, I follow contemporary Greek New Testament editions, which place this line as the concluding one in verse 7.

20. The final line (v. 8c) reproduces Bockmuehl's phrasing (*Philippians*, 139). This fifth line is an "additional" line for any construal of stanzas, illustrating Mark Keown's point that the hymn or poem "is not written with perfect symmetry" (*Philippians*, 1:370).

But in this case, it is Christ's humanity that is highlighted, with *anthrōpos* repeated.[21]

A further connection between stanzas occurs in their third lines (7a, 8a), which employ two indicative verbs paired in both cases with the reflexive pronoun "himself" (*heauton*). Christ "emptied himself" (*kenoō* [7a]) and "humbled himself" (*tapeinoō* [8a]).[22] Additionally, each of these two lines is followed by a line containing a participle of means. Christ "emptied himself *by taking* [*labōn*] the form of a slave"; and he "humbled himself *by becoming* [*genomenos*] obedient to death."

I suggest that these macrolevel poetic patterns across Philippians 2:6–8 signal that Paul has moved into poetry and also indicate something of the shape of the poem so far (namely, its initial paired stanzas). A frame or *inclusio* is also evident in the final stanza of the poem, verses 9–11. The focus on Christ's exaltation, after his acts of self-emptying and self-humbling, is communicated by the repetition of theme in 9a and 11b:

> **9a** Therefore **God raised him to the place of highest honor**
> **9b** and graced him with the name that is above every name,
> **10a** that at the name of Jesus every knee will bow,
> **10b** in heaven and on earth and under the earth,
> **11a** and every tongue will profess that Jesus Christ is Lord
> **11b** **to the honor of God the Father.**

God's action of honoring Christ in the utmost way (9a) (which is the establishment of Christ's lordship [11a]) results in God's own honor being acclaimed (11b). While different terms are used

21. First in the plural and then in the singular; see discussion below.

22. Both of these lines are fairly short when compared to the previous two in their stanzas. Zogbo and Wendland suggest that readers of poetry "take note of a poetic line (colon) that is exceptional or breaks some established pattern, for example one that is overly long or short" (*Hebrew Poetry*, 41). Such breaks in pattern can indicate a marked element of the text/poem.

to express raising to the place of honor (*hyperypsoō* [9a]) and honor or glory (*doxa* [11b]),[23] the repetition of these closely related ideas, along with the repetition of *theos* ("God"), frames this stanza as a unit and signals God's action of bestowing honor on Christ after his self-humbling.

### *Poetic Lines: Microlevel Connections*

In addition to seeing macrolevel poetic envelopes, patterns, and repetitions, we can also zoom in to notice what is going on line by line in Philippians 2:6–11, in order to see if the passage fits poetic conventions at this level. First, Hebrew (Semitic) poetry tends toward a simple clause structure and is characterized by something called "parataxis."[24] Parataxis involves avoidance or minimal use of conjunctions between clauses or lines. Consider Julius Caesar's well-known line: "I came, I saw, I conquered." This is parataxis.[25] And it is a common feature of the Christ poem; only a third of the lines of the verses 6–8 begin with conjunctions. Additionally, the initial lines of both *stanzas* exhibit parataxis (6a, 7c). Although some have argued that the *kai* ("and") of 7d provides a clear break between ideas,[26] in a poem we could expect a stanza to begin without a conjunction, which is precisely what we see at 7c: "being made in the likeness"—in other words, parataxis.[27] Within the first two stanzas of the poem, consisting of eight or nine lines, there are only three conjunctions introducing lines (7a, 7d, 8c).

23. The use of synonyms in poetry is commonplace (see discussion under "Careful Use of Language" below).

24. Dobbs-Allsopp includes "simple clause structure [and] parataxis" among the key features of Hebrew poetry (*Biblical Poetry*, 9).

25. In Latin: *Veni, vidi, vici* (Hirsch, *Poet's Glossary*, 43).

26. And, consequently, starts a new stanza, or, for those identifying this passage as prose, a new sentence or clause (e.g., Fee, *Philippians*, 214–15; see also Silva, *Philippians*, 106).

27. For an example from the Psalms, see the stanza that begins in Ps. 1:4 (MT and LXX), with no initiating conjunction.

When conjunctions are used in paratactic discourse—which includes poetry—conjunctions that indicate coordination rather than subordination are preferred. This means that we could expect to see judicious use in poetry of such conjunctions as "and" (*kai*, *de*) and "but" (*alla*, *de*), since these connect coordinating lines. This is, in fact, what we do see in Philippians 2:6–8, where the only conjunctions that Paul uses are *alla*, *kai*, and *de* (in 7a, 7d, 8c, respectively). Even in 2:9–11, where a few subordinate conjunctions are used (*hina* in 10a; *hoti* in 11b), the structure of these lines remains fairly simple and straightforward, with coordinating lines and conjunctions dominating: *dio kai* ("therefore" [9a]) and *kai* ("and" [9b, 11a]; see also within 10b).[28]

Another feature of Jewish poetry—one that fits the simple clause structure already mentioned—is the use of parallelism in adjacent lines. Parallelism involves a balancing of form and ideas between adjacent lines. This has traditionally been understood as a standard characteristic of Hebrew poetry. While categories and definitions have been contested, it is relatively easy to spot examples of pairs of balanced lines across Old Testament poetry, featuring corresponding elements with either similar meanings ("synonymous parallelism") or contrasting ideas ("antithetical parallelism").[29]

Parallelism or use of balanced lines occurs across the poem of Philippians 2. The poem begins with what seems to be an example of antithetical parallelism between its first two lines (6a // 6b).

> **6a** Who, though being in the form of God,
> **6b** did not consider equality with God as something to be exploited;

28. David Winston identifies as Hebraic (or "Hebrew coloring") "the simple connection of clauses by conjunctions such as *kai*, *de* . . . , *dia touto*, *dio*, *gar*, and *hoti*" (*Wisdom of Solomon*, 15), which he then refers to as "paratactic structure" (15n3).

29. An example of synonymous parallelism can be seen between the two lines of Ps. 100:2; antithetical parallelism is illustrated by Prov. 12:5.

While there is not an exact pattern of parallel features between the two lines, two of three elements in each are closely aligned: the verbs "being" and "did not consider" (contrasting ideas) as well as the parallel ideas "in the form of God" and "equality with God."[30] The pointed contrast between these lines involves Christ's determination not to exploit what he already was or the status he already had ("in the form of God").[31]

Two examples of synonymous parallelism occur in the third stanza of the poem (2:9–11). The first pair of lines, which begins this section, is relatively easy to spot.

> **9a** Therefore God raised him to the place of highest honor
> **9b** and [God] graced him with the name that is above every name,

The second set of parallel lines comes in 10a and 11a, although it is interrupted by an added phrase: "in heaven and on earth and under the earth" (10b). We can see that 10b is an addition, since the two lines surrounding it are taken directly from the Greek translation of Isaiah 45:23b. In Isaiah, Israel's God, Yahweh, claims to be the rightful recipient of universal worship and acknowledgment: "to me every knee will bow and every tongue will acknowledge God" (LXX translation). We can see the parallel elements of these two lines by removing for a moment the inserted language of 10b:

> **10a** that at the name of Jesus every knee will bow,
> **11a** and every tongue will profess that Jesus Christ is Lord

In addition to noticing the two sets of paired elements ("knee" and "tongue"; "bow" and "profess"), we can see that the first line

30. Bockmuehl, *Philippians*, 126.

31. The debate over the meaning of *morphē theou* is vigorous and lengthy. For an extended treatment, see Fabricatore, *Form of God*.

begins with reference to Jesus and "the name" and the second line concludes similarly: Jesus as Lord ("the name" of Israel's God [see below]). Paul has quoted from Isaiah and heightened the universal lordship of Jesus by adding that every entity "in heaven and on earth and under the earth" will bow the knee to Jesus Christ.

There is one more instance of parallelism in the Christ poem, which I have left for last. I've done so even though I consider it to be the clearest example of poetic parallelism in the entire poem: lines 7c and 7d. I have left these synonymous lines for last because their relationship has been obscured or complicated by the history of English Bible translation going back at least to the King James Version (KJV). Here is how the 1611 version of the King James arranges these lines:

> 6 Who being in the forme of God, thought it not robbery to bee equall with God:
>
> 7 But made himselfe of no reputation, and tooke vpon him the forme of a seruant, and was made in the likenesse of men.
>
> 8 And being found in fashion as a man, he humbled himselfe, and became obedient vnto death, euen the death of the Crosse.

Two important facets of the KJV have impacted a great many translations (and some Greek New Testament editions) up to the present. The first issue is the versification of the KJV, which separates the two parallel lines ("was made in the likenesse of men. / And being found in fashion as a man") into different verses.[32] The second issue is the punctuation and sentence divisions, which, again, place a full stop after the first line (7d) and its potential pair (8a). The sentence structure of the KJV indicates that the

32. Contemporary Greek New Testament editions uniformly place both lines in verse 7.

first line (7d) goes with what precedes and the second (8a) with what follows.

These interpretive decisions have significantly impacted the history of translation and interpretation of the Christ poem. Even as many modern translations identify this passage as poetry (e.g., formatting with poetic lines), the majority follow the KJV in tying the first line back to 2:6–7 and the second line to what follows in 2:8 (e.g., CSB, CEB, NLT, NRSVue). Additionally, some translations continue to include that second line in verse 8 (e.g., NKJV, NIV), so that the chance of seeing the poetic parallelism is significantly diminished.

We can take a close look at these two lines and observe their parallel features. Each substantive element of the first line finds a corresponding element in the second, whether through use of synonyms (the verbs and datives) or direct repetition ("human being[s]").

> **7c** Being made in the likeness of human beings
> **7d** and being found in appearance as a human being[33]

Yet the parallelism in Philippians 2:7c and 2:7d has been masked or discounted, not only by choices of versification and punctuation but also by a key semantic argument. That argument goes like this: In parallel lines, we would expect the second line to add something new to the meaning of the first. But in 2:7, there is virtually no difference between the two lines in terms of their semantic content or meaning. Gordon Fee, who has been influential in arguing that 2:6–11 is "exalted prose" rather than full-blown poetry, suggests that grouping these two lines together in poetic parallelism creates "a nearly intolerable redundancy."[34] He also notes that "this kind of identical parallelism (where two

33. With the Greek reading: 7c *en homoiōmati anthrōpōn genomenos* / 7d *kai schēmati heuretheis hōs anthrōpos*.

34. Fee, *Philippians*, 203n43.

synonymous lines say exactly the same thing) would not only be unique for this passage, but cannot in fact be found elsewhere in Paul."[35] For Fee, this "intolerable redundancy" is readily alleviated by understanding 7d to begin a new extended clause (splitting it apart formally and semantically from 7c).[36]

Yet I suggest that there is less redundancy between the two lines than Fee and others have assumed. In my reading, the second line builds on and extends the idea of the first rather than merely repeating it. The first line introduces the incarnation—Christ becoming human—by allusion to Genesis 1:26–27.

> Being made in the likeness [*homoiōma*] of **human beings** [*anthrōpoi*] (Phil. 2:7c)

> Let us make **humanity** [*anthrōpos*] according to our image and likeness [*homoiōsis*] (Gen. 1:26a LXX)

Paul draws on the language of humanity created in God's *likeness* from Genesis 1 to refer to Christ's incarnation—his coming in the *likeness* of humanity.

The second paired line in the Christ poem does not simply restate the first. Instead, it moves from the general notion of Christ's incarnation—"being made in the likeness of human beings"—to a specific reference to his human experience. Paul proceeds from general to specific by moving from the plural for humanity (*anthrōpoi*, "human beings") in the first line, to the singular in the second—a particular human being (*anthrōpos*).[37]

35. Fee, *Philippians*, 214n3.

36. Fee also suggests that the *kai* functions better as a connection between two participial clauses than between two parallel lines (*Philippians*, 214n3). Yet in the LXX of Psalms, *kai* routinely functions to join parallel synonymous lines (often translating the Hebrew initial *waw*). See, for example, Pss. 1:1–3; 2:3–5; 3:5, 9 (ET 3:4, 8); cf. also Wis. 9:2–12.

37. In Gen. 1:27b and 1:27c, we can observe a similar though not exactly identical use of parallelism, in that case moving from singular ("that [human] one") to

[7c] Being made in the likeness of human beings
[7d] and being found in appearance as a particular human being

Susan Eastman explains how the singular "human being," along with the dative noun, *schēmati*, functions as a particularization of the previous line, not just its repetition. Her translation of 2:7d illustrates this movement from general to particular: Christ is found "in the trappings of a singular human being."[38] Eastman's insight helps us to recognize how the second line expands on the first. As I note in my commentary on Philippians, "The singular form ('human being' rather than the plural) extends the idea from Christ's incarnation in solidarity with humanity to the particular expression his humanity took—that is, a Jewish man born into a world shaped by Roman power and might. Though the poem does not specify these particulars, the first half [of the poem] does conclude with a reference to crucifixion (2:8), a specifically Roman form of execution."[39]

This reading receives further confirmation from Markus Bockmuehl, who notes that the verb within the second line, "found" (*heuriskō*), is used here to refer to "the way a person's circumstances turn out in the event, rather than what is the case in principle."[40] The message of the Christ poem is that "in Christ,

---

plural ("them") pronouns.

And God made the human,
according to the image of God he made *that one*,
male and female he made *them*. (LXX [my translation])

38. Eastman, "Philippians 2:6–11," 2. Later in her analysis she notes that "the body is the site of revelation; physical existence is the place where Christ's true identity . . . is displayed" (12). This fits Ralph Martin's reading that the verb + dative ("being found in appearance") "denotes the external appearance of the incarnate Son as He showed Himself to those who saw Him in 'the days of his flesh'" (citing Heb. 5:7) (Carmen Christi, 207).

39. Brown, *Philippians*, 120.

40. Bockmuehl, *Philippians*, 138. Fowl also reads these two lines together and notes that they "describe the earthly manifestation of Christ's decision to give up his exalted position in favor of one of obedience" (*Story of Christ*, 59–60).

his death and resurrection, God's original design for humanity finally achieved *concrete shape and fulfillment*."[41]

We began by exploring macrolevel structural clues that Philippians 2:6–11 is poetry. Now, we have noticed microlevel connections that imply the same, including four sets of parallel lines along with the passage's relatively simple clause structure and its parataxis. Two additional clues that point toward poetry can be covered more briefly. The first is concision and careful language choices. The second is the presence of figurative speech and sound devices.

### *Careful Use of Language*

In addition to structural and line features, *concision* is a key element of Jewish poetry.[42] The concise nature of poetry means that quite a lot is communicated in relatively few words. In Philippians 2:6–11, we hear the entire story of the Messiah in a brief, carefully worded vignette. In short order, we hear of the movement from preexistent unity in the Godhead to Christ's identification with humanity, to his willingness to experience a slave's execution, to his resulting exaltation and glorification to the highest place.[43] The entire story of the Messiah is here "compacted . . . into poetic lines."[44]

Along with economy of words, poets also tend to be very thoughtful in their word choices. Poetry "generally uses fewer words than prose, but the words are carefully chosen. . . . Poets select words with great care for their aesthetic appeal as well as

41. Dunn, "Christ," 79 (italics added).

42. Dobbs-Allsopp, *On Biblical Poetry*, 9.

43. If we compare the various passages about exemplars in Philippians 2 and 3, we gain a sense of the relative economy of words used in the Christ poem. Paul uses 76 words to show Jesus as exemplar in 2:6–11, while the clearly prose descriptions of Epaphroditus and Paul himself as exemplars are given 103 and 121 words, respectively. Only the brief prose sketch of Timothy's example roughly matches (72 words) the word count of the Christ poem, and, in that case, Paul provides fairly limited information about Timothy.

44. Whitlock, "New Testament Poetry," 87 (describing poetry in Acts).

their content."[45] Such judicious word selection could account for the variety of language in the Christ poem, with some of its terms not used by Paul elsewhere in his writings (i.e., quite a few *hapax legomena*). For example, the following terms are used by Paul only in this passage:

- *morphē* ("form" [vv. 6, 7])
- *harpagmos* ("something to be exploited" [v. 6])
- *isa* [*theō*] ("equality [with God]" [v. 6])
- *hyperypsoō* ("raise to the place of highest honor" [v. 9])
- *katachthonios* ("under the earth" [v. 10])

Additionally, Bockmuehl observes that Paul nowhere else refers to "Christ's incarnation in terms of 'self-humbling' (via *kenoō*, v. 7; *tapeinoō*, v. 8)." He goes on to suggest, "It is precisely in poetical or lyrical contexts that one might well expect an author to resort to unusual language."[46]

Unusual language and a general preference for synonyms rather than strict repetition of the same word (except to signal poetic structure) is an important feature of poetry.[47] Noticing this feature can explain Paul's use of a variety of synonyms for his depiction of Christ, including *morphē* ("form"), *homoiōma* ("likeness"),

45. Brown, *Scripture as Communication*, 145.

46. Bockmuehl, *Philippians*, 118. See Keown's even fuller list of words and phrases in 2:6–11 that are "unique, unusual, or uncommon in Paul" (*Philippians*, 1:353).

47. Brown, *Philippians*, 109; Fowl, *Philippians*, 111. Such variation might seem, at first glance, to contravene what we noted previously about the frequent use of repetition in poetry, especially to signal structural interconnections. Yet it is this dual reality—the push and pull of variation and repetition—that characterizes poetry. Dobbs-Allsopp refers to this dual reality of repetition with variation in his description of poetic form involving "a repetition riven . . . by variation and equivalence" (*Biblical Poetry*, 109). Elsewhere, he describes this kind of repetition with variation as follows: "The patterned repetition that generates formal structure . . . will routinely involve a host of diverse linguistic elements (e.g., lineation, sound play, parallelism, word repetition) distributed in a variety of overlapping and mutually informing and delimiting ways" (192).

and *schēma* ("appearance") in verses 6–8. Given the amount of ink spilt on the finely tuned nuances of each of these terms (whole books have been written on *morphē* alone), it can be helpful to recognize that these words are more alike than different and that pressing fine points of distinction among them could potentially be a genre misstep.[48] As Moisés Silva proposes, "It would be difficult to prove that if these three terms were interchanged, a substantive semantic difference would result."[49]

### *Sounds and Figures of Speech*

Biblical poetry is also characterized by use of sound devices and figurative speech. Repetition of sounds and of words is often heightened in poetry, and we can see instances of sounds and words recurring in the Christ poem, including the following:

- the framing of the first stanza with *morphē theou* and *morphē doulou* (2:6a, 7b)
- the threefold repetition of "name" language: *to onoma* [name] *to hyper pan onoma* [name], *hina en tō onomati* [name] *Iēsou* (2:9b–c)
- the repeated end sounds (assonance): *epouraniōn kai epigeiōn kai katachthoniōn* ("in heaven and on earth and under the earth") (2:10b)

Metaphor and imagery, while used in a variety of genres, "is particularly pervasive in poetry."[50] The Christ poem centers on

48. Hawthorne and Martin affirm that the three terms "form a threefold reiteration of the one fundamentally important idea: Christ in the incarnation identified himself with humanity" (*Philippians*, 120). As Paul Minear suggests, the Christ poem "has often been distorted by an overemphasis on dogmatic substance; music [i.e., poetry] is not the place to look for theological precision" ("Singing and Suffering," 204). For the general pattern of liberal use of synonyms in poetry, see Brown, *Scripture as Communication*, 146.

49. Silva, *Philippians*, 115 (see also 106).

50. Brown, *Scripture as Communication*, 139.

one particular metaphor, that of Christ taking on the "form of a slave." This metaphor comes at a crucial moment in the poem and is accented in a couple of important ways: through sound device and its placement at the end of the first stanza. The sound resonance between the stanza's first and last lines accents the metaphor: Christ's movement from *morphē theou* (6a) to *morphēn doulou* (7b).

> **6a** Who, though being in the form of God [*morphē theou*],
> **6b** did not consider equality with God as something to be exploited;
> **7a** rather, he emptied himself
> **7b** by taking the form of a slave [*morphē doulou*].

The metaphorical nature of this image is clear since the human existence of Christ was not one of physical (literal) slavery.[51] This metaphor seems best read as identifying Jesus' incarnation (his becoming human) without being pressed to equate human existence with a slave's existence. Instead, Paul uses *doulos* as a metaphor to show "a jarring juxtaposition" between Christ's original status ("in the form of God") to his status as human being ("taking the form of a slave").[52]

Assigning the metaphor of slave to Christ "was to assign to him a position of greatest opprobrium in the social world of Paul's readers."[53] In Philippi in the mid-first century, the language of *doulos* was, as Joseph Hellerman suggests, "socially charged"

51. Bockmuehl offers a nuance that the image communicates that Christ was "a metaphorical slave" rather than that he was "like a literal [slave]" (citing Moule, "Further Reflections," for the simile view) (*Philippians*, 155).

52. Brown, *Philippians*, 118. The metaphorical function of [*morphē*] *doulos* in no way requires the earlier instance of [*morphē*] *theos* to be metaphorical. Fee sees the two as both indicating the "essential quality" of what it meant to be God and, alternatively, as slave (*Philippians*, 211). James Dunn speaks of the double function of *morphē* and then notes, "Such a double function of a term is precisely what one might expect in poetic mode" ("Christ," 77).

53. Hellerman, *Reconstructing Honor*, 142.

and held "negative connotations . . . for persons preoccupied with honor and social status in Roman Philippi."[54] Slaves existed on the lowest status rung of society, even if some of them enjoyed certain privileges associated with a wealthy or influential household.[55] This base social status provides the most likely reason for Paul's use of the slave metaphor, especially in light of the reference to divine status that begins the stanza. Paul visualizes for his audience "the steep descent of Christ in status from 'the form of God' to the 'form of a slave.'"[56]

Another potent image in the Christ poem comes in the concluding and climactic line of verse 8: "all the way to death on a cross." Although not itself a metaphor (since Christ was crucified), the image of a cross (*stauros*) would have had significant *symbolic resonance* in first-century Philippi. Crucifixion was a specifically Roman form of execution and was associated with slavery. It was the form of execution used for criminals and slaves and was "the most shameful public humiliation" in that context.[57] These associations certainly would have been felt by the Philippian audience, as Paul narrated the descent of the obedient Christ to the lowest and most dishonorable place imaginable.

## The Significance of Philippians 2:6–11 as Poetry

If Philippians 2:6–11 is poetry, what difference does it make to read it as such? What would it mean to adjust our genre expectations as we move from the prose of Paul's exhortations in 1:27–2:4 to the Christ poem? Moisés Silva suggests that 2:6–8 falls into two stanzas (as I have argued) and then makes this caveat: "Whether or not such an arrangement puts us in touch with

54. Hellerman, *Reconstructing Honor*, 139, 136.
55. Hellerman, *Reconstructing Honor*, 139.
56. Brown, *Philippians*, 118; see Bird and Gupta, *Philippians*, 79.
57. Hellerman, *Reconstructing Honor*, 143.

the original structure of the hymn, it is certainly suggestive and may have a bearing on exegesis."[58] Silva affirms that whether or not any particular reconstruction is "precisely accurate," such reconstruction is "exegetically useful."[59] Making the shift in our genre expectations from prose to poetry at 2:6 is, indeed, exegetically useful. What we notice when we attune our ears to the poetic cadences of this passage can help us better understand what Paul is communicating through the poem.[60] As we review the whole poem, we can summarize its contours and its communicative force.

6a Who, though being in the form of God,
  6b did not consider equality with God as something to be exploited;
7a rather, he emptied himself
  7b by taking the form of a slave.

7c Being made in the likeness of human beings
  7d and being found in appearance as a particular human being,
8a he humbled himself
  8b by becoming obedient to death,
  8c all the way to death on a cross.

9a Therefore God raised him to the place of highest honor
  9b and graced him with the name that is above every name,
10a that at the name of Jesus every knee will bow,
  10b in heaven and on earth and under the earth,
11a and every tongue will profess that Jesus Christ is Lord
  11b to the honor of God the Father.

58. Silva, *Philippians*, 99.

59. Silva, *Philippians*, 93.

60. Dunn suggests, "The fact of the matter is that too much of the debate on the exegesis of this passage has displayed rather crass artistic or literary insensitivity" (referring to sensitivity to recognizing allusions in the text) ("Christ," 75).

The first stanza follows the story of Christ from his original status through "the steep descent" that occurred when he became human,[61] with "slave" (*doulos*) as a metaphor for that lowest point of descent from Christ's divine status. As Peter Oakes comments, "Between being like God and being like a slave, there is the widest status gap imaginable by Paul's hearers."[62] This stanza is framed by the *morphē* ("form") language that in each case begins the Greek line: *en morphē theou* (6a) to *morphēn doulou* (7b). The first (positive) action of Christ is provided in this stanza: "he emptied [*kenoō*] himself"—a phrase that echoes Paul's admonition in 2:3 for the Philippians to avoid "vain conceit" (*kenodoxia*). That noun shares the root of the verb "empty," used in 2:7. This connection signals that Christ's self-emptying involved his "divestiture of position,"[63] which fits the downward trajectory of status already built into the stanza's frame.

**6a** Who, though being in the form of God,
  **6b** did not consider equality with God as something to be exploited;
**7a** rather, he emptied [*kenoō*] himself (cf. *kenodoxia* [2:3])
  **7b** by taking the form of a slave.

The second stanza picks up where the first leaves off. And it moves through an increasingly granular depiction of Christ's journey as a human being.[64] The stanza begins with the two parallel lines that echo God's creation of humanity in Genesis 1:26–27. As

61. Brown, *Philippians*, 118.
62. Oakes, *Philippians*, 196.
63. BDAG, 539.
64. Another insight arising from taking the poetry of this passage seriously is a greater flexibility for the narrative flow of the poem. Viewing this text as prose can tend toward reading a "strict progression of thought" across it, "insist[ing] that each line says one thing and one only; and that in logical order" (Martin, Carmen Christi, 194). Poetry, even a poem with a story backbone like the Christ poem, should not be held to such a strict temporal sequence.

humanity was made in God's likeness, Christ is made in humanity's likeness. Susan Eastman suggests that we see here a grand reversal: Christ "assimilating to Adamic humanity in a mirror reversal of Adam's creation in the likeness of God."[65]

> 7c Being made in the likeness [*homoiōma*] of human beings [*anthrōpoi*] [cf. Gen. 1:27]
> 7d and being found in appearance as a particular human being [*anthrōpos*],
> 8a he humbled himself
> 8b by becoming obedient to death,
> 8c all the way to death on a cross.

The Genesis resonance in the first paired line is followed by a particularization of the incarnation. In other words, the second line moves from a general recognition of Christ's identification with all humanity to his "being found in appearance as a particular human being" (2:7d)—in Eastman's words, "in the trappings of a singular human being."[66] Jesus' specific identity—"a Jewish man born into a world shaped by Roman power and might"—is hinted at in the lines that follow.[67]

Christ's action in response to his human state was to humble himself even further.[68] Just as Christ's action of *kenōsis* or emptying (*kenoō* [2:7a]) finds a counterpart in Paul's exhortations for the Philippians to eschew "vain conceit" (*kenodoxia* [2:3]), so too his self-humbling (*tapeinoō* [2:8a]) meets Paul's earlier call to "humility" (*tapeinophrosynē* [2:3]). Christ's humbling of himself is identified with his faithful obedience that extended even to his

65. Eastman, *Paul and the Person*, 137.

66. Eastman, "Philippians 2:6–11," 2.

67. Brown, *Philippians*, 120. Bird and Gupta note the "generic quality" of the poem until 8c (with its reference to a "cross") (*Philippians*, 82). I understand the particularization to begin already in 7d, however subtly.

68. Oakes notes that "humbled" governs the two participles of 7c and 7d (*Philippians*, 120).

willingness to die (2:8b). The movement of the stanza continues toward greater particularity in its crescendo to the kind of death experienced by Christ—"death on a cross" (2:8c). Here, the poem "crashes into vivid historical reality with the word 'cross.'"[69] As already noted, the image of a Roman cross would have had negative associations of public humiliation, being the form of execution most often reserved for slaves and criminals.

Not only does this final line of the first half of the Christ poem land on the most particularized expression of Christ's choice to become human; it also provides the climactic moment of the entire poem so far. Christ's emptying himself of the highest status meets his self-humbling all the way to the cross. Both form and content combine to emphasize this last line as the depths of Christ's "downward mobility."[70] In terms of form, this line provides an additional, fifth line to the second stanza and so receives weight and emphasis.[71] Markus Bockmuehl notes that the line "is in some ways the odd one out: the literary rhythm appears to slow down and grind to a halt at this point."[72] The slowing rhythm is met by the rhythmic repetition of sound from line 8b to 8c: "to death, all the way to death on a cross"—in Greek, *mechri thanatou, thanatou de staurou.*

The content of the final line also contributes to its emphasis. Bockmuehl suggests that the slowing down of the poem's rhythm here matches the poem's content: "The literary rhythm appears to slow down and grind to a halt at this point. So, of course, does the narrative of Christ's descent and death."[73] As the pace of the Christ hymn slows to match the descent of the Christ story in

69. Bird and Gupta, *Philippians*, 82.

70. Eastman, "Philippians 2:6–11," 17.

71. In the threefold stanza configuration for 2:6–8, this final line is an addition line as well (making the final, third stanza a four-line instead of three-line stanza). In other words, in both configurations this line stands out.

72. Bockmuehl, *Philippians*, 125. He goes on to highlight "the special status of this line as the pivot and turning point between the two halves" of the poem (125–26).

73. Bockmuehl, *Philippians*, 125.

all its particularity, our vision is directed with laser focus on the epitome of Christ's self-emptying and self-humbling: his missional death on a Roman cross. It seems to me that the Christ hymn, especially at this crucial turning point, fits Robert Alter's description of a biblical poem that centers on "a predicament . . . that is amplified from verset to verset and from line to line. Poetic form acts in these cases as a kind of magnifying glass, concentrating the rays of meaning to a white-hot point."[74] In the poem of Philippians 2, the cross (*stauros*) becomes a white-hot point—the lowest moment of Christ's descent and the height of his human faithfulness and obedience.

In the final stanza, Paul narrates an amazing turn of events, the reversal of Christ's descent: from slavery to lordship, from the depths of shame to the heights of honor.

> **9a** Therefore God raised him to the place of highest honor
>    **9b** and graced him with the name that is above every name,
> **10a** that at the name of Jesus every knee will bow,
>    **10b** in heaven and on earth and under the earth,
> **11a** and every tongue will profess that Jesus Christ is Lord
>    **11b** to the honor of God the Father.

We have already noticed the repetition of "name" (*onoma*) language and the recurring motifs of "highest" and "above all" as well as "honor" and "glory." We have also noted that Paul draws a set of parallel lines from Isaiah 45:23 (lines 10a and 11a in the Christ poem) and inserts an explanatory and rhythmic line between them—"in heaven and on earth and under the earth"—all to

74. Alter, *Art of Biblical Poetry*, 76. In context, Alter is addressing the "focusing" effect in some Jewish poetry: "There are . . . many biblical poems in which any implied events, even metaphoric ones, are secondary while what is primary is a predicament, an image, or a thematic idea that is amplified from verset to verset and from line to line. Poetic form acts in these cases as a kind of magnifying glass, concentrating the rays of meaning to a while-hot point."

accent the universal lordship that Christ is now accorded through his God-given "place of highest honor." Yet to be examined is the significance of Christ's exaltation in light of the naming motif that Paul employs and his use of a citation from Isaiah 45.

It is crucial to observe that Isaiah 45:23 (the text Paul cites) comes at the conclusion of a long polemic against all competitors to Israel's God. Across Isaiah 45, we hear this monotheistic refrain:[75] "I am the LORD, and there is no other" (45:5–6, 18; cf. vv. 21–22 [NIV]; similarly, in the LXX). In the Septuagint, the "Lord" (*kyrios*) translates "YHWH" from the Hebrew, the divine name. And the Lord, who has been speaking across Isaiah 45, now claims the divine prerogative of universal lordship: "To me every knee will bow and every tongue will acknowledge God" (45:23 LXX). Only Yahweh, the one true God, deserves worship from every creature.

So, what does this mean for the Christ poem? Paul was most certainly aware of the profound emphasis on the uniqueness of Yahweh in Isaiah 45 that culminates at verse 23. And he deploys this Isaiah citation to affirm that Jesus the Messiah is worthy of universal acclaim and worship. Notice what Paul does here: he places Jesus squarely in the place of universal lordship—a place reserved for Israel's God alone. And this transposition of YHWH's universal authority to Jesus makes clear that "the name that is above every name" is precisely the divine name: "Lord."[76] We hear this in the substitution at the end of the citation: "every tongue will profess that *Jesus Christ is Lord* [*kyrios*]."[77] As Richard Bauckham expresses it, "The exaltation of Jesus [is] his identification as YHWH in YHWH's universal sovereignty."[78]

75. Or at least a refrain that emphasizes *monolatry*—i.e., worship of Yahweh alone without a corresponding denial of the existence of others gods. For the debate around the use of monotheism, monolatry, and other such terms vis à vis ancient Judaism, see, for example, Heiser, "Monotheism."

76. In Hebrew, *YHWH*; in Greek (LXX and New Testament), *kyrios*.

77. With *theos* ("God") in the LXX replaced by "that Jesus Christ is Lord" (*hoti kyrios Iēsous Christos*) in Philippians.

78. Bauckham, *Jesus and the God of Israel*, 38.

The poem that began with Christ at the heights of divine status has shown his willingness to give up that status to become human, and beyond that to embrace a death of disgrace on a Roman cross. Because of his willing obedience to the greatest extent, God has exalted him to the *highest* place of honor and given him the name above every name: the name "Lord" (YHWH). Yet the lordship of Jesus Christ—the acknowledgment and worship that he does and will receive—is only the penultimate moment of the poem. We hear in the final line the ultimate point to which Christ's identity and work have led: "to the honor of God the Father" (2:11b). As God has raised Christ "to the place of highest honor," so Christ's exaltation after his faithful journey results in honor given back to God the Father. The poem ends by focusing attention on the divine unity (cf. 1:2).

## The Function of the Christ Poem in Philippians (and the Influence of Philippians on the Poem)

In chapter 1, I introduced the notion of bidirectional influence between an embedded genre and its macrogenre. Sune Auken suggests that "embedded genres are transformed by their new generic context, but features are carried over from the original genre specifically to influence this new context."[79] Although interpretation of embedded genres rightly focuses on the latter side of the equation (how the embedded genre impacts its context), it can be hermeneutically profitable to explore how an embedded genre is transformed by its macrocontext. We begin with this less obvious direction of influence: how the Christ poem has been impacted by its placement in the letter. Here I am less concerned about reconstructions of what a possible preexisting poem or hymn may have looked like before Paul brought it into

79. Auken, "Genres inside Genres," 186.

its current context in Philippians 2,[80] and more interested in the question of how the macrogenre of letter may have influenced the poem and its use.

Paul's placement of the poem signals how his paraenetic or persuasive emphasis—a hallmark of the epistolary genre[81]—informs his use of the poem. In Philippians 1:27–2:4, we hear Paul exhorting the Philippians toward a set of actions and dispositions, some of which he will assign poetically to Christ (e.g., humility [2:3, 8]). Additionally, in 2:5–3:17, Paul places before his audience some key exemplars for them to emulate: Christ (2:5–11); Timothy (2:19–24); Epaphroditus (2:25–30); and Paul himself (3:1–17). The Christ poem is shaped by the epistle genre, in that it is used in the Philippian letter to provide the first and premier example that believers are to follow.

The prose line that introduces the Christ poem makes clear this connection to the letter and to its paraenetic function: "Have this mindset among you which was also in Christ Jesus" (2:5).[82] Christ's story, expressed in poetic form, provides a paradigm for believers to follow, even as they pattern their lives analogously, rather than exactly, after Christ's.[83]

Yet even as the function of the Christ poem is impacted by its paraenetic context, the poem's lyrical shape and features contrib-

80. These not insignificant questions were prominent areas of focus in early form-critical studies of the "Christ hymn" (e.g., Jeremias, "Zu Phil ii 7").

81. Letters, at their heart, usually include ideas, exhortations, and encouragements, "bolstered by argumentation and other rhetorical supports" (Brown, *Scripture as Communication*, 152).

82. There are two distinct ways of reading 2:5. The kerygmatic reading interprets the clipped phrase "which also in Christ Jesus" (*ho kai en Christō Iēsou*) as referring to the mindset that believers already possess in Christ (e.g., "Have this mind among yourselves, which is yours in Christ Jesus" [RSV]). The ethical reading interprets this phrase as Christ's own mindset, which provides the example for believers to emulate. For further discussion and an argument for the latter reading, see Brown, *Philippians*, 111–12. Either reading allows for a paradigmatic focus.

83. Stephen Fowl offers the language of analogy and explains, "Christians participate in the economy that Christ reveals, but their participation is guided by analogy rather than isomorphic imitation" (*Philippians*, 106–7).

ute *poetically* to the Philippian letter. An initial way we see this poetic contribution is through what we can imagine would have been a deep and holistic engagement with its audience. We hear in 2:5 that Paul intends the poem to contribute to the development of a Christ-like mindset (*phronēma*) that impacts the whole person and the entire community. I suggest that this kind of whole-person response is what Paul desires for the Philippian church precisely as he moves to poetry. Recall for a moment my daughter's deeply experienced and whole-person response to "I Dreamed a Dream." Paul may very well use the Christ poem to engender that kind of whole-person responsiveness. Paul Minear, who views the Christ poem of Philippians 2:6–11 as a sung hymn, suggests this kind of holistic impact on the Philippians: "The hymn functioned in such a way as to shape the *phronēma* of the congregation and to clarify its sense of vocation. Emerging from deep levels of communal experience, the song articulated in both verbal and musical terms a rich cargo of non-verbal affections and emotions."[84]

Although exploring how texts tap into affections and emotions can be difficult to gauge with any precision, this area of analysis offers real and important considerations that invite interpretive exploration. Here we are moving into the terrain of *pathos*, an important area of ancient rhetoric, involving "the emotions and tendencies that can be expected of an audience."[85] David deSilva frames the entire interpretive task (involving attention to *logos*, *ethos*, and *pathos*)[86] as "identifying and entering into the inner argumentation of the text, discerning varying kinds of appeal that make the text an address to the 'whole person' of the hearer (i.e., to his or her mind, feelings, and connection with the speaker)."[87] This whole-person engagement is something that the genre of

84. Minear, "Singing and Suffering," 205.

85. Cunningham, Compier, and Boyce, "Classical Rhetorical Tradition," 18.

86. For an overview of these three core areas of rhetoric and their application to epistolary interpretation, see Brown, *Philippians*, 30–32.

87. deSilva, "Appeals," 247.

poetry does particularly well: "Using sound and form creatively and with care, poets woo us and captivate us. Poetry draws us into a place of whole-person responsiveness."[88]

A crucial way that the Christ poem contributes to the Philippian letter is *doxological*—it evokes a response of praise. Here, we can return to the long-standing view that Philippians 2:6–11 is a Christian hymn. While it is difficult to prove that this text functioned as a hymn in the early church and formed the basis for Paul's adaptation, we can with confidence affirm at least one key facet of its hymn-like quality: it praises the one whom it places in the spotlight. As Gerald Hawthorne and Ralph Martin suggest, "The center of gravity of the hymn is a carefully constructed tribute—an 'encomium,' a tribute of praise . . . in honor of Jesus Christ, who is now elevated to share the Father's throne and is universal Lord."[89] This is a *genre* contribution of the Christ poem. Although the exhortations and affirmations that a letter provides could, at points, draw its audience into praise, a poem—especially one that focuses on Jesus Christ as Lord as Philippians 2 does—has this intended response of doxology hardwired into it.[90]

By moving to poetry in his letter to the Philippians, Paul invites a whole-person response involving both worship of Jesus as Lord and emulation of Jesus as humble *doulos*. These two portraits and responses are integrally connected in the poem. For the way that *Jesus is Lord* provides an utterly different paradigm of lordship than the Philippian congregation would have experienced within their own political and theological milieu. As N. T. Wright describes, at the center of the poem "is a celebration of *the radically different kind of lordship* attained, and now

88. Brown, *Scripture as Communication*, 145.

89. Hawthorne and Martin, *Philippians*, 133.

90. For a discussion of the hermeneutics of this idea of intended response (the text's perlocutionary intention), see Brown, *Scripture as Communication*, 21–24, 101–5.

exercised, by Jesus."[91] And this radical "downward mobility" that defines the story of Jesus provides the path for the Philippian congregation to embrace the same mindset and live as an alternative community marked by humility and service, and, indeed, by worship.

91. Wright, "Joy," 52 (italics added).

THREE

# Is Jesus a Riddler in Matthew?

## *The Role of Riddles in the Gospel of Matthew*

Riddles are told for fun—at least in my own cultural context. A riddle I heard often when growing up was, "What is black and white and red [read] all over?" Answer: a newspaper. Here's another: "I'm tall when I'm young, and I'm short when I'm old. What am I?" Answer: a candle.

It probably goes without saying that riddles are most often culturally specific.[1] And, at least in my Western (United States) context, there's not much at stake in telling and answering riddles. Their goal is entertainment—the pleasure you feel when you "get it right." There is not much at stake in *not* guessing the correct answer to a riddle.

1. For example, Chinese riddles have higher stakes, with shame and honor being attached to their telling, especially in larger groups (personal communication with Chao Ma, June 2, 2022).

Yet consider that folklorists have identified what are called "neck riddles"—a type of riddle that requires a person to use their wits to answer it, in order to elude danger, or to "save their neck."[2] With a neck riddle, the stakes are high—very high. And in the first-century world in which Jesus lived, riddles often had higher stakes than we might initially suspect.[3] At stake in the making and answering of riddles are honor and shame, a demonstration of superior wisdom, and sometimes life and death. It is no coincidence that Jesus engages with the Jerusalem leaders in a contest of riddles (Matt. 21–22) just days before his execution at their instigation (see 26:15). In this chapter, we will address these questions: Does Matthew portray Jesus as a Messiah who riddles? And, if so, how might this help us interpret the Gospel of Matthew?

## Riddles and Other Embedded Genres in Matthew

Matthew's Gospel has quite an array of embedded genres—various forms that populate this writing that, at the macrolevel, is a biography about Jesus.[4] Matthew as a biographer incorporates his own diverse set of subgenres, including an opening genealogy (1:1–16), quite a number scriptural fulfillment quotations, and various narrative forms, defined in specific ways by form critics of a previous era, such as pronouncement stories and controversies. But the greatest number of embedded genres occur *within* the teachings of Matthew's Jesus, illuminating the diversity of forms that Jesus used as he communicated "the good news of

2. Abrahams and Dundes, "Riddles," 133. See also Thatcher, *Riddles of Jesus*, 219; Crenshaw, "Riddle," 749. "Neck riddles" within northern Europe and in some African traditions "are generally framed by the story of the man who saved his neck by the exercise of his wit, by propounding a riddle his executioner could not answer" (Abrahams and Dundes, "Riddles," 133).

3. Compare Samson's riddle and the devastating results of its answer being divulged in Judg. 14.

4. Burridge, *What Are the Gospels?*

the kingdom" in his public ministry. Robert Stein identifies quite a variety of teaching forms that Jesus used, including parable (7:24–27),[5] poetry (7:7), proverb (13:57), hyperbole (5:29–30), metaphor (5:13), pun (16:18), and riddle.[6]

In this chapter I will tap into that last category—the riddle—to see if Matthew portrays Jesus using riddles, and even using riddles routinely. To put it more provocatively, In Matthew, is Jesus a Messiah of riddles? I will seek to demonstrate that Matthew's Jesus often does use riddles to teach about the arriving kingdom, his own identity, and the way of discipleship as well as to evade tests and tricks set up for him by his opponents.

But why look for riddles? Why of all the subgenres employed by Matthew's Jesus do I choose to explore riddles? A primary reason is that riddles are not often the subject of interpretive conversations in the Gospels. We could say that, generally speaking, they are *underidentified and so underinterpreted*. It is common enough to hear it affirmed that Jesus' teachings were not always easy to understand, but the fault for this is usually placed at the feet of his listeners. The problem is those dull and obdurate disciples. Or we blame the religious and political leaders Jesus comes in contact with for their inability to grasp what we can plainly see—who Jesus was and what he was about.

But what if, at least sometimes, Jesus was intentionally ambiguous? As we will soon see, intentional ambiguity is at the heart of a riddle. If Jesus, at least some of the time, communicated cryptically *by design*, this would help to explain the many different types of responses to him. Now, the notion that some of Jesus' teachings have some amount of ambiguity is not new to Gospels study, especially as Jesus used such a variety of teaching forms.

5. Jesus' parables form a central core of his teaching and in Matthew provide important touchpoints, especially within the five great discourses across the Gospel, which together contain some fifteen parables.

6. Stein, *Method and Message*.

A story (parable) can be ambiguous. Hyperbole can be ambiguous. A pun can be ambiguous. Metaphor can be ambiguous. But a riddle is different: few other teaching forms are, *by definition*, ambiguous. No other teaching form is, *at the heart of it*, deliberately ambiguous.

It is my contention that the use of riddles by Jesus has not been adequately explored. It is true that many Gospels scholars give a general nod to the presence of riddles within the teachings of Jesus, many times within lists of the varieties of kinds of material that he used to teach. A half century ago, Joachim Jeremias suggested that, unlike the teachings of Jesus' contemporaries, there are a "considerable number of . . . riddles in Jesus' teachings."[7] Yet, to my knowledge, the only scholar to dive deeply into this possibility and its interpretive implications is Tom Thatcher, first in an exploration of riddles in John and then in his study of riddles in all four Gospels.[8] The dearth of scholarship on this topic contributes to an underidentification of riddles in the Gospels.

Another reason riddles are underidentified involves the lack of clear formal indicators for many riddles. As Thatcher points out, "*The things that make a statement a 'riddle' are not always things that you can see or hear in the statement itself.*"[9] What defines a riddle as riddle has significant cultural parameters[10] and, in many contexts, is tied less to formal than to functional qualities—that is, what a riddle does to and for its speaker and hearer. Those of us, at least from Western contexts, will need to think beyond

7. Jeremias, *New Testament Theology*, 30. He notes, "Teachers of [Jesus'] time did not teach in this way and the early church did not invent riddles . . . for Jesus. On the contrary, it clarified them" (31). Ivor Jones mentions the "metaphorical imagery which is everywhere to be found in the synoptic material, in aphorisms and Wisdom, as in logia and riddles" (*Matthean Parables*, 107n21).

8. Respectively, *The Riddles of Jesus in John: A Study in Tradition and Folklore* (2000) and *Jesus the Riddler: The Power of Ambiguity in the Gospels* (2006).

9. Thatcher, *Jesus the Riddler*, xix.

10. Thatcher, *Jesus the Riddler*, xv.

our narrow category of riddle, with its "What is . . . ?" or "What has . . . ?" set up. We will also need to disabuse ourselves of the idea that riddles are all fun and games—puzzles told primarily or exclusively for their entertainment value.

Yet the reality that riddles can lack formal indicators means we could fall into the trap of finding *a riddle under every rock*. If riddles are ambiguous, this doesn't mean that every point of ambiguity within Jesus' teachings indicates he is speaking in riddle. We'll need some criteria for determining riddles in the Gospels—something Thatcher provides for us in his work. And I'll add some of my own parameters for discerning the riddles of Jesus in Matthew.

In the end, identifying whether something in Jesus' teachings is a riddle has interpretive significance. This is the key reason I have been intrigued by this subgenre in Matthew. I have found that identifying riddles in Matthew makes a difference for the interpretation of the riddle and, at times, the larger section of which it is a part. At the chapter's conclusion, I will suggest some reasons why Matthew's Jesus riddles as he does.

## Defining and Identifying Riddles

As we move to define and identify riddles in Matthew, it can be helpful to place Jesus' riddles within their wider context by looking to the Jewish Scriptures. In the Hebrew Bible, riddles fit within a larger category of *māšāl*—an umbrella term that, as R. T. France notes, "covers proverbs . . . , fables, prophetic utterances, and even riddles, as well as allegorical parables like those of Ezekiel."[11] The Greek word *parabolē* essentially covers the same ground as *māšāl*. In fact, the Hebrew *māšāl* typically is translated by the Greek

11. France, *Matthew*, 502. See also Stein, *Method and Message*, 34–35. Ben Witherington highlights the broad scope of *māšāl*, noting that it "includes everything from one-liners to riddles to full-fledged parables" (*Jesus the Sage*, 19).

*parabolē* in the Septuagint.[12] So, *parabolē* has a wider referent than what we think of when we hear the English word "parable."[13] This is true for Matthew's use of *parabolē*, which sometimes identifies a saying (e.g., a riddle) rather than a story (e.g., Matt. 15:15).[14]

With this lexical information in hand, let's consider what riddles are and how we might identify them. Thatcher describes riddles as "confusing on purpose."[15] His definition highlights *intentional ambiguity* and focuses on the multiple potential referents of a riddle: "A 'riddle' is an interrogative statement that intentionally obscures its referent (the thing or idea that it is talking about) and asks the audience to name it. Riddles obscure their referents through controlled ambiguity, the artful use of language that could reasonably refer to more than one thing."[16] To return to a shorter definition, James Crenshaw describes a riddle as "a saying that both puzzles the hearers and communicates to them."[17] What these definitions have in common is the theme of ambiguity.

The newspaper riddle mentioned at the start of this chapter is one that works only as a spoken (not a written) riddle: "What is black and white and red all over?" Answer: a newspaper. The ambiguity of this riddle arises from the use of "red," which, immediately

12. France, *Matthew*, 502.

13. BDAG, 759. We can see this wider meaning of *parabolē* in Matthew's parables chapter (13:1–53). Matthew explains why Jesus speaks in *parabolai* (the plural form) by referencing Ps. 78:2: "I will open my mouth in parables [*parabolē*], I will announce things that have been hidden from the foundation of the world" (Matt. 13:35 [my translation]). In the Hebrew of the psalm, the term used for "hidden things" (Ps. 77:2 LXX: *problēmata*; Matt. 13:15: *kekrymmena*) is *ḥîdâ*, meaning a "riddle." In this Matthean citation, *parabolē* and *kekrymmena* ("hidden thing" or "riddle") are set in synonymous parallelism, suggesting they are similar or overlapping categories.

14. Any number of commentators tie the parables of Matt. 13 closely to riddles. For example, Craig Keener notes that when Jesus teaches only in parables (with no accompanying explanation), he "*offers riddles whose answer can be fathomed only by those who understand the riddles in the context of his own ministry*" (*Matthew*, 379). Ulrich Luz posits that the parable of the wheat and the weeds may have been understood as a "riddle parable" by the church (*Matthew 8–20*, 255).

15. Thatcher, *Jesus the Riddler*, 3.

16. Thatcher, *Jesus the Riddler*, 3.

17. Crenshaw, "Riddle," 749.

preceded by the mention of the colors black and white, is likely to be heard initially as referring to a third color. Only upon hearing the answer (or knowing it from previous tellings) does the hearer understand that they should hear "read"—the act of reading, passive voice—instead of the color. The riddle—this "artful use of language"—plays on different referents.[18]

Let's look at a riddling question from Matthew's Gospel. After Jesus bestows forgiveness on a man who is paralyzed (9:2), his antagonists accuse him of blasphemy (9:3). Jesus asks a question that seems to be a riddle: "Which is easier, to say, 'Your sins are forgiven,' or to say, 'Rise and walk'?" Both questions can provide the "right" answer to "Which is easier to say?"—something commentators routinely note. Presumably, in an era where healers were plentiful enough, healing is an easier feat than granting forgiveness, since only God can do the latter. The scribes in the story clearly consider this a theological issue since they accuse Jesus of "blasphemy" (9:3). Yet it would be easier to *say*—that is, to pronounce—forgiveness than healing, since verification of a healing would be immediately obvious (or not). Rodney Reeves, who identifies this question as a riddle, notes, "It was much easier to say, 'Your sins are forgiven' since who can tell if it's true?"[19]

Yet riddles are not necessarily formal questions. Thatcher's definition identifies a riddle as "an interrogative statement."[20] This point of nuance means that riddles have the quality of a question, without necessarily involving the formal feature of an interrogative (i.e., being shaped as a question). As anthropologist Elli Köngäs Maranda notes, "The riddle image is always conceptually a question, be it syntactically interrogative or not."[21]

A riddle of Jesus that implicitly offers a question can be found in Matthew 22:21. In response to a trick question about whether

18. Or in this case, different meanings of the homophone "red/read."
19. Reeves, *Matthew*, 188.
20. Thatcher, *Jesus the Riddler*, 3.
21. Maranda, "Riddle Analysis," 54.

it is right to pay the imperial tax (22:15–17), Jesus poses a riddle. After pressing his antagonists to produce the appropriate coin and to identify whose image and inscription are on it, Jesus says this: "Give to Caesar what belongs to Caesar, and to God what belongs to God."[22] Routinely, commentators refer to this saying as "cryptic,"[23] "oblique,"[24] or, as Ben Witherington puts it, "deliberately ambiguous."[25] It is, I suggest, a riddle.[26]

Although this saying is not a question grammatically, it functions interrogatively, since the hearer is required to sort out what belongs to Caesar and what belongs to God. In fact, it is the ambiguity of these two referents—*ta Kaisaros* ("what belongs to Caesar") and *ta tou theou* ("what belongs to God")—that puts this aphorism squarely in the category of a riddle. Additionally, Thatcher's insight that riddles "play with the audience's sense of order and values" is on full display in this particular saying, as Jesus questions any neat division between what belongs to Caesar and what belongs to God.[27] We will explore this riddle more fully later in the chapter, but for now we can note that, strictly speaking, the form of a question is not a requirement of a riddle.

So far, we know this much: riddles are intentionally ambiguous statements or questions, but always with an interrogative sense to them. How do we go about identifying riddles in a larger work like the narrative of Matthew? In other words, how do we locate riddles as an embedded genre? If we think that a saying or question is a riddle, is there a way to confirm or authenticate that identification? Thatcher helps us again by providing

22. Across this chapter, I use my own translation for Matthew's Gospel (from Brown and Roberts, *Matthew*). For other biblical texts, the NIV is used.

23. Brown and Roberts, *Matthew*, 487; Davies and Allison, *Matthew*, 3:218 ("relatively cryptic").

24. Senior, *Matthew*, 248.

25. Witherington, *Matthew*, 413.

26. Brown and Roberts, *Matthew*, 203, 487.

27. Thatcher, *Jesus the Riddler*, 15.

a set of potential criteria for identifying riddles, which I have adapted to some extent based on my own analysis of riddles in the Gospels.

The first two criteria arise directly from the definition of riddles: their ambiguity and their interrogative sense. We may be hearing a riddle if an ambiguity in the saying can be adequately clarified or "solved" by *multiple referents*. As we saw in Matthew 9:5, the easier thing to say could be alternatively construed as proclaiming healing or announcing sins forgiven. Both alternatives are possible, and so Jesus may be offering a riddle. A second criterion involves the presence of an interrogative quality. We may be hearing a riddle if the line is framed directly as a question (as in Matt. 9:5), or if it has an interrogative sense to it. In other words, a riddle "*leaves it to the audience to resolve the dilemma*."[28] We heard this interrogative flavor (though not form) in Matthew 22:21 ("Give to Caesar . . . , and to God . . ."), since with this alternative Jesus sets an implicit choice before his audience.

These two basic criteria move us toward identifying a riddle without yet having a narrative context to aid and assist. But in Matthew we benefit from the literary context, and so we can identify a number of narrative cues to confirm we are dealing with a riddle.[29]

The first set of cues that a riddle is being told are provided *by the narrator*. In other words, the Gospel writers themselves often signal to the reader the presence of a riddle. Thatcher offers a Johannine example of an extended narrative aside identifying a riddle of Jesus. In John 10:6, we read, "Jesus used this figure of speech [the image of a good shepherd], but the Pharisees did not understand what he was telling them."[30] In most cases, however, cues offered by the Gospel narrators are not this direct

28. Thatcher, *Jesus the Riddler*, 48.

29. These are adapted from Thatcher, *Jesus the Riddler*, 48–49; and *Riddles of Jesus*, 181–82.

30. See Thatcher, *Riddles of Jesus*, 181.

or extensive. In Matthew, narrative cues frequently involve just a single word. For example, Matthew uses *pagideuō* at 22:15 to indicate the intention of certain Jewish leaders to "trap" Jesus by offering a trick question.[31] It is not surprising then that Jesus uses a riddle—in this case, the Caesar/God riddle—to elude their trap (22:21). A narrator can also signal the presence of riddles by framing a section of text as a "riddling session,"[32] an extended set of questions, tests, and contests in which riddles play a central role. As we will soon see, much of Matthew 21–22 (and specifically 21:23–22:46) is a riddling session, and we will spend some time walking through this extended set of vignettes to highlight where and how riddles are used. At this point, we can note that Matthew gives multiple, often subtle cues that this passage is a riddling session, including his choice of language for how various groups of Jewish leaders approach and interact with Jesus.

Another point of confirmation that a riddle is being used comes *from speakers themselves*,[33] and, for our purposes, indications Jesus gives that he is "riddling." While not all questions Jesus asks are riddles, and not all riddles are shaped in the form of a question, making particular note of questions can be fertile ground for identifying potential riddles. Additionally, Thatcher notes that riddles sometimes are introduced by stock questions and phrases, like the introductory question "What do you think?" (Matt. 17:25; 21:28; 22:17, 42; cf. 18:12) and the aphorism "The one who has ears ought to listen" (Matt. 11:15; 13:9, 43).[34] Both of these occur in Jesus' speech in Matthew. General calls by the Matthean Jesus to "listen" and "understand" are also potential markers of

31. Thatcher identifies this question as a riddle (*Jesus the Riddler*, 40–41). Reeves suggests that the questioners in 22:15 are "trying to force Jesus into a no-win situation, a first-century catch 22" (*Matthew*, 437).

32. See Thatcher, *Jesus the Riddler*, 49.

33. Thatcher, *Jesus the Riddler*, 48.

34. Thatcher, *Jesus the Riddler*, 40–41 and 30–31, respectively.

riddles or enigmatic sayings (e.g., Matt. 15:10; cf. 19:12).[35] Other speaker cues include providing an indirect answer to a question posed or even a deferral of an answer. In Matthew 21:23–27, for example, Jesus avoids answering a question from his adversaries by refusing to answer their question unless they answer his first.

A final lens for confirming a riddle comes *from the audience in the story*.[36] If narrative characters respond to a particular saying or question with some amount of confusion, it could be that they are reacting to a riddle.[37] In a similar vein, when listeners hear Jesus teaching and register amazement, this may also suggest a riddle has been spoken (e.g., Matt. 22:22, 33). We can observe a riddle signaled by audience confusion in Matthew 15. There, Jesus responds to a question by some Pharisees and scribes about his disciples not participating in purity washings (15:1–2) by giving this aphorism: "It is not what enters the mouth that defiles a person, but it is what comes out of the mouth that defiles a person" (15:11). In response, the disciples report to Jesus that the Jewish leaders "stumble over" the aphorism Jesus has spoken (15:12). And the disciples themselves are confused by what Jesus has said, so that Peter needs to ask for an explanation of this *parabolē* (15:15). These responses suggest that Jesus has told a riddle.[38] We can note a similar confusion on the part of the disciples in Matthew 16:5–13, when Jesus warns them of the "yeast of the Pharisees and Sadducees" (v. 6). They are bewildered and think that Jesus is speaking about physical bread (v. 7), whereas he is warning them about the influence (the teaching) of these Jewish leaders (vv. 11–12).[39]

35. Riesner, *Jesus als Lehrer*, 375.

36. Thatcher, *Jesus the Riddler*, 48.

37. Thatcher, *Riddles of Jesus*, 181.

38. As identified by Schnackenburg, *Matthew*, 148; on the parallel in Mark 7:15, see also Stein, *Method and Message*, 157n26; Witherington, *Jesus the Sage*, 95.

39. Those who understand 16:6 to be a riddle include Thatcher, *Jesus the Riddler*, 56; Luz, *Matthew 8–20*, 250.

## The Riddling Session of Matthew 21:23–22:46

A riddle "involves a match of wits in which the individual is challenged to discover the concealed meaning" of the riddle.[40] In this match of wits, "the riddler wins if the riddlee can't answer."[41] When the "match of wits" is extended to include more than a single riddle, we can identify the prolonged contest as a "riddling session." Roger Abrahams and Alan Dundes, in their study of riddles in various cultures, describe riddling sessions as "special occasions during which [riddles are] used in a properly playful contest situation."[42] While in some social contexts riddles are used, as these authors note, in playful ways, in other cultural contexts riddling sessions raise higher stakes of honor and shame. This is true of the first-century social context, which often is described as an "agonistic society"—defined by "its intensely competitive nature."[43] Such competition shows up in the regular "public challenges . . . put to [Jesus] throughout his career."[44] The stakes for riddling are high in Matthew because first-century society attributed great value to riddles and riddling.[45]

### *Identifying the Riddling Session*

The engagement narrated in Matthew 21–22 between Jesus and various groups of Jewish leaders in Jerusalem offers an extended riddling session, in which questions, tests, and contests predominate and where riddles play a central role.[46] A riddling session begins at Matthew 21:23 with the question posed to Jesus about the source of his authority, and the session runs through the end of

40. Stein, *Method and Message*, 18.

41. Thatcher, *Jesus the Riddler*, 4.

42. Abrahams and Dundes, "Riddles," 130. As Thatcher notes, "All riddles are . . . agonistic to some degree, meaning that they involve a sort of competition" (*Jesus the Riddler*, 3–4).

43. Neyrey, *Honor and Shame*, 16.

44. Neyrey, *Honor and Shame*, 16.

45. Thatcher notes that what and how much is at stake depends on the "value . . . a particular culture attributes to riddling" (*Jesus the Riddler*, 4).

46. This is the definition for a riddling session that I have offered above.

chapter 22, where Jesus (finally!) provides his answer to that initial question (22:41–46). Across this riddling session, we encounter the various riddle criteria: (1) intentional ambiguity on Jesus' part that presses his hearers to make a choice (i.e., it has an interrogative form or at least sense) and (2) additional literary cues from the narrator, the speaker, and the hearers that indicate a riddle is occurring. Matthew portrays Jesus as the wise sage, who can both answer and elude the verbal traps set for him. As W. D. Davies and Dale Allison describe Jesus' answers to his opponents across 21:23–22:46, "They are uniformly creative and clever, memorable and colourful; and they avoid entanglement either by turning a question back on others . . . or moving the discussion to another level."[47]

### *The Framework for 21:23–22:46: Jesus' Authority Questioned and Answered*

After Jesus enters Jerusalem in messianic fashion and interrupts the commerce happening in the temple (21:1–17), the Jewish elders and chief priests question his authority for these actions: "By what authority are you doing these things? And who gave you this authority?" (21:23). When Jesus defers answering their question, a riddling session is set in motion that runs across the rest of chapters 21–22. Various groups of Jewish leaders bring questions and tests to Jesus, and he, at every turn, bests them at their own game. In the end, Jesus asks the final question and poses a riddle that silences them all. Matthean scholars line up to agree that Matthew 22:43–45—Jesus' reply to the leaders' answer that the Messiah is David's son—is a riddle:[48]

> How does David by the Spirit call him "Lord," when he says:
> "The Lord said to my Lord,
> 'Sit at my right hand,

47. Davies and Allison, *Matthew*, 3:168–69. They suggest 21:23–22:46 as a discrete unit.

48. See scholars listed in note 80 below.

> until I put your enemies
> under your feet'"?
> So if David calls him "Lord," how can he be his son?

This riddle posed by Jesus answers the initial question about the source of his authority (21:23). The answer? His is the highest authority—he is lord even over his ancestor David. Together, the initial question and the final answer frame the entire riddling session.

### *Walking through the Riddling Session*

Between the initial question challenging Jesus' authority and his riddle that finally answers that question is an extended riddling session. We will walk through Matthew 21:23–22:46, with an eye to the riddles that fuel the competing claims for authority between Jesus and the Jerusalem leaders.

#### Matthew 21:23–27: Initial Dueling Questions

When asked about the source of his authority by the chief priests and elders, Jesus answers with a question of his own. As Donald Hagner notes, their questions are "an attempt to gain more ammunition to be used against Jesus when the time is right."[49] Jesus' rejoinder sets up a binary, with two opposite answers possible: "I will also ask you one question. If you answer it for me, then I will tell you by what authority I am doing these things. Where did John's baptism come from—from heaven or from humans?" (21:24–25).

The question Jesus asks sets up a "catch-22" for the Jerusalem leaders, and it moves the focus away from Jesus to John the Baptist (a smart move!). If they answer that John's baptism came from God, then they indict themselves for having rejected John's mes-

49. Hagner, *Matthew*, 609.

sage (21:25). If they answer in the negative, they lose favor with the crowds who consider John a prophet (21:26). So, they avoid answering altogether and respond, "We don't know." Jesus has already bested them at the game of questioning by avoiding answering their questions about his authority, which were intended to trap him. He has deferred an answer—at least for the time being.

The riddling session is initiated with a set of questions lobbed back and forth and with no one getting or giving a direct answer. There are no riddles as of yet, but the contest of wits has begun, with Jesus successfully eluding their initial trap.

### Matthew 21:28–32: The Parable (or Is It a Riddle?) of Two Sons

Jesus goes on the offensive at this point and takes charge of the dialogue. Conventionally, the next three pericopes are identified as story parables: the parables of the two sons (21:28–32), the vineyard (21:33–44), and the wedding feast (22:1–14). And Matthew indicates that each of these should be understood as a *parabolē* (21:33; 22:1). Yet, as we have seen, *parabolē* should not simply be equated with the more narrowly defined English word "parable"—a simple story told to illustrate a lesson and to impact an audience. Instead, *parabolē* can refer to an array of sapiential forms, including riddles.

Hermeneutically important for the first *parabolē* is its introductory question, "What do you think?" As we have seen, this stock question can signal a riddle.[50] The potential riddle consists of a scenario (21:28–30) culminating in a binary question (21:31):

> A man had two sons. He came to the first and said, "My son, go and work in my vineyard today." The son replied, "I do not want to go," but later he changed his mind and went out. The father came to the other son and said the same thing. That son replied, "I will go, sir," but he did not go. *Which of the two did the will of the father?*

50. Thatcher, *Jesus the Riddler*, 40–41.

On the face of it, this question seems to have an easy answer, which the Jewish leaders provide: "The first" (21:31).[51] And we can assume that Matthew would concur, given that "doing the will of the Father" (*to thelēma tou patros*) is a significant Matthean motif (7:21; 12:50; 21:31). We can also note that, in Jesus' subsequent accusation (21:31–32), his opponents provide a direct contrast to the first son, who has a "change of mind" (*metamelomai* [21:29]) and so ends up obeying his father. Jesus accuses them, "You did not change your minds [*metamelomai*] and come to believe John" (21:32).

Yet there is ambiguity in the question "Which of the two did the will of the father?" (21:31), since the first son initially defies his father's request—a culturally unacceptable action in that social context and potentially a cause for shame and disgrace.[52] As we hear in the Jewish writing Sirach, written in the second century BCE, "Honor your father by word and deed, that his blessing may come upon you" (3:8 NRSVue). And in Matthew, the importance of congruence between words and deeds has already been signaled in chapter 12: "By your words you will be vindicated, and by your words you will be condemned" (12:37). Teasing out the inherent ambiguity of the question "Which of the two did the will of the father?" we can view both sons as partially disobedient. As Kevin Barker puts it, "Disobedience intermingled with obedience is still disobedience in some measure."[53] The ideal response would be a "yes" response in both word and deed, which neither son provides. Yet this ideal, both/and obedience is the ultimate point of the passage. Given the disobedience (in

51. Reeves calls it a simple parable and "not much of a riddle at all" (*Matthew*, 425).

52. Wendell Langley notes the first son's "absence of respect," although he suggests that this first son "stops somewhat short of actively insulting his father" ("Parable of the Two Sons," 233). See also Hagner, *Matthew*, 613; Thatcher, *Jesus the Riddler*, 54.

53. Barker, "Two Sons," 62. Barker comments, "Right belief results in right attitude and right attitude results in right speech and right action."

some measure) of both sons, the question Jesus asks seems to be a riddle.[54]

The riddle-like quality of this *parabolē* is further supported by the text-critical jumble it produced after its composition. One relevant text-critical issue has to do with how the Jewish leaders answer the question about which son did their father's will. The manuscript evidence suggests the original answer was "The first" (*ho prōtos*). Yet at least some scribes substituted "The last" (*ho eschatos*),[55] "potentially because of the dishonor that would have been perceived to attend to the first son's (initial) refusal to obey his father."[56] Scribal confusion may suggest that this first *parabolē* of Jesus is a riddle.

We can summarize the riddling session explored thus far. It began with a question (21:23)—a challenge by the Jerusalem leadership to Jesus' messianic actions as he entered Jerusalem and the temple (21:1–17). Jesus responded with his own question for these leaders, which left his questioners in a quandary. Now, Jesus has spoken a riddle to indict them for their rejection of John's message (21:32). This riddling session is winding up to be the "ultimate turf war," as Rodney Reeves puts it.[57]

## Matthew 21:33–22:14: Two Parables of Indictment (That Include a Riddle)

Matthew narrates Jesus confronting the Jewish leaders with two more *parabolai*, the parable of the vineyard (21:33–46) and the parable of the wedding feast (22:1–14), both indicting these leaders for their rejection of Jesus as "son." While neither of these *parabolai* itself is a riddle, there is at least one riddle used within

54. Or, as Langley frames it, "a choice between two viable alternatives" (key to the definition of a riddle) ("Parable of the Two Sons," 234).

55. This is a Western reading, included in Codex D and some Old Latin and Syriac translations.

56. Brown and Roberts, *Matthew*, 198n14.

57. Reeves, *Matthew*, 421 (referring to 21:23–22:14).

them. After telling the first of these two parables, Jesus cites Psalm 118, about the rejected stone, to highlight the theme of the son's rejection (Ps. 118:22–23 in Matt. 21:42).[58] He then indicates that the kingdom will be taken out of the hands of the Jewish leadership because of their rejection (21:43). Now comes the riddle: "The one who falls on this stone will be dashed to pieces, and the one on whom it falls will be crushed" (21:44).[59] This saying is elusive enough to fit the categorization of riddle, with its open-ended personal referents (who is being referred to as "the one" in each clause?) and the use of a rare and obscure final verb, *likmaō* ("crush" or "scatter"?).[60] A look at Matthean commentaries shows that it is a difficult saying to interpret.[61]

### MATTHEW 22:15–40: THREE TRICK QUESTIONS IN RAPID SUCCESSION

Jesus has told three *parabolai* in a row to incriminate the Jerusalem leadership—identified specifically as the chief priests, elders of the people, and Pharisees (21:23, 45)—for their rejection of his messianic authority. Now, the leaders go on the offensive, as they had attempted to do in their initial question (21:23). Three groups, each in turn, approach Jesus with trick questions, intending to trap him by the answers he gives (22:15, 34–35). Here we will look at each one in turn.

*Matthew 22:15–22: A riddle about paying the imperial tax*. The first question comes from an unlikely alliance between Pharisees

58. The son of the parable and the son who is Jesus.

59. Witherington identifies 21:44 as a riddle (*Matthew*, 406).

60. BDAG, 596.

61. For example, Luz notes that the verse "is not easy to interpret" (*Matthew 21–28*, 43). Additionally, its presence is textually uncertain, which raises at least the possibility that scribal confusion over its riddle-like qualities caused some scribes to omit it. Another proposal comes from France, who suggests that its awkward placement (a step removed from the Ps. 118 quotation) might explain its omission (*Matthew*, 807n3). If it is secondary, the likeliest explanation is a harmonization with Luke 20:18.

and Herodians (22:15–16). These leaders, who likely held opposing views on the question of paying Roman taxes, ask Jesus if it is lawful to pay the imperial tax to Caesar (22:17). Their question seems intended as a catch-22, since answering either yes or no would alienate some part of the social landscape in first-century Judaism. In fact, Thatcher categorizes the question itself as a riddle.[62] If Jesus responds by suggesting that paying the imperial tax is something a faithful Jewish person should do, he risks alienating all those sympathetic to revolutionary currents against Roman occupation. If he answers otherwise, he could be pegged as a revolutionary himself and a threat to Rome (as is made explicit in Luke 20:20).[63]

But Jesus is not so easily fooled. He doesn't answer with a clear yes or no; instead, he performs a riddle. First, Jesus asks his opponents to produce a denarius (the cost of the tax), and to confirm whose image and inscription are on the coin (22:19–20). Then he tells them, "Give to Caesar what belongs to Caesar, and to God what belongs to God" (22:21). Although framed as a clear binary between the realms of Caesar and of God, the reality is far more complicated. Intentional ambiguity signals that the saying is a riddle.[64] First, an important Jewish conviction affirms that all things belong to God. Consider, for example, Psalm 24: "The earth is the Lord's, and everything in it" (v. 1). On the Roman side of things, Caesar's claims were also all encompassing. This would have been palpably visible on the denarius that Jesus and his inquisitors were viewing, which read on one side (in Latin) "Tiberius Caesar Augustus, son of the Divine Augustus," and

62. In reference to its Markan parallel in Mark 12:14 (Thatcher, *Jesus the Riddler*, 57). If their question is a riddle, it could fit Thatcher's category of an alternative riddle: "a riddle that attempts to force the riddlee to choose between two or more proposed answers, all of which would be embarrassing and/or dangerous" (96). It might also fit the category of a neck riddle, which "the riddlee must answer correctly or suffer pain, death, or public humiliation" (8).

63. Brown and Roberts, *Matthew*, 486.

64. Witherington refers to verse 21 as "deliberately ambiguous" (*Matthew*, 411).

on the other side "High Priest" to describe Caesar.[65] Through his riddle, "Jesus can implicitly assert Yahweh's universal rule in the face of Rome's claims to sovereignty, yet avoid falling into his opponents' trap by directly eschewing payment of the imperial tax."[66]

We have already noted that one of the corroborating criteria for identifying riddles is an audience's confused or astonished response. In Matthew 22:22, we hear that Jesus' opponents are amazed. This response suggests that, at a minimum, they are impressed with his capacity to evade their trap. Viewed more broadly, it implies that they experience some amount of bewilderment at Jesus' words.[67] Matthew has framed the entire pericope to identify the riddle Jesus tells within it—from the laying of a trap for Jesus (22:15) to the amazement of his trappers in the end (22:22).

*Matthew 22:23–33: The riddling Sadducees.* Matthew ties the next contest of wits closely with the one about the imperial tax. He does this by using a temporal marker ("that same day") and noting that another group within the Jerusalem leadership comes with a question (22:23). The Sadducees provide what they think is a ridiculous scenario to show how preposterous belief in resurrection is (since this group did not hold to belief in resurrection [22:23; cf. Acts 23:7–8]). Both David Garland and David Turner identify the entire scenario as a riddle—from the hypothetical account of a woman married successively to seven brothers, to its concluding question about whose wife she will be in the resurrection.[68] After seeing another set of leaders bested by the riddling Jesus, these Sadducees bring a riddle of their own to him.

Their question, "At the resurrection, whose wife from among the seven will she be?" (22:28), is meant to reveal an absurdity,

65. See Perrin, *Jesus the Priest*, 243–47.

66. Brown and Roberts, *Matthew*, 203.

67. The term that Matthew uses, *thaumazō*, indicates being "extraordinarily impressed or disturbed by something" (BDAG, 444); cf. Matt. 21:20.

68. Garland, *Reading Matthew*, 224; Turner calls it "a sort of riddle-parable" (*Matthew*, 530).

signaling that a wife with seven (resurrected) husbands provides an insurmountable obstacle for the whole notion of resurrection. Yet Jesus is not baffled by this riddle, although he doesn't directly answer their question about whose wife she will be, which has no right answer to it. So he evades their direct question and goes on the offensive by pointing out their fundamental error regarding the resurrection itself. He accuses, "You are deceived because you don't know either the Scriptures or God's power" (22:29). He then corrects these Sadducees about the nature of final resurrection, its basis in the Torah, and the very God they claim to trust (22:31–32). Garland suggests that their error is theological: "The Sadducees have underestimated God."[69]

As Jesus outwits his opponents once again, Matthew indicates that the crowds—who have been listening in (see 21:8–11, 26, 46)—are "amazed at his teaching."[70] Once more, we can look to audience response to confirm that this episode in Matthew is part of a riddling session.[71]

*Matthew 22:34–40: Prioritizing Torah commandments.* The next line of attack by the Jerusalem leadership comes from a Pharisee described as a Torah expert, who is commissioned when the Pharisees hear that Jesus had "silenced the Sadducees" (22:34–35). This introduction to the final of three questions lobbed at Jesus emphasizes three realities about this riddling session. First, the three questions are asked to test or trap Jesus. The imperial tax question was intended as a trap (22:15: *pagideuō*; cf. 22:18: *peirazō*). The

69. Garland, *Reading Matthew*, 224.

70. Here Matthew uses the verb *ekplēssō*, which, according to BDAG (308), can be defined as "to cause to be filled with amazement to the point of being overwhelmed" (e.g., "dumbfounded"). The same term is used to express the crowds' amazement at Jesus' teaching (7:28), his hometown's astonishment at his wisdom and powers (13:54), and his own disciples' response to his teaching (19:25). As will be discussed below, Jesus' wisdom often enough defies comprehension.

71. Although Jesus' entire response is not a riddle, his comparison between people in the resurrection and angels has a riddle-like quality (an ambiguous metaphor). As already noted, the Sadducees have told a riddle in this scene.

Sadducees pose a riddle meant to make Jesus' belief in resurrection look ridiculous. And now this Torah expert is out to test him (22:35: *perirazō*).[72] Notice also that each question is framed as a Torah question, from "Is it lawful . . . ?" (22:17), to the Sadducees' question surrounding the Torah-prescribed levirate marriage (22:24), to the question of the greatest commandment (22:36). Jesus' reputation as a legitimate teacher of the Torah has been on the line in each case.

A final point: it is worth noting that going on the offensive against Jesus has created some strange bedfellows among the Jewish leaders in Jerusalem. Jesus offends the chief priests and scribes with his actions in the temple (21:15), and it is the chief priests and elders of the people who bring the initial question to Jesus about his authority for this action (21:23). After Jesus' initial two *parabolai*, the chief priests and Pharisees recognize that he is referring to them (21:45). Then, in quick succession, three groups approach Jesus to trick him: Pharisees along with Herodians (22:15–16), Sadducees (22:23), and Pharisees once again (22:34–35; cf. 22:41). These different groups have distinct loyalties and views; they disagree on much. But they come with a united front to catch Jesus in his words.

In the final test, the delegated Pharisee asks Jesus for his understanding of the "greatest commandment in the law" (22:36). While Matthew indicates that the query is meant to test Jesus, this question, on its surface, is not an obvious trap.[73] Gary Burge suggests, "Jesus is presented with a classic dilemma of law. Surely not all laws could be equally important: some must be 'weighty,' others 'light.'"[74] Burge goes on to note that the "danger in [this] sort of

72. Matthew identifies earlier "tests" (using the verb *peirazō*) given by the devil (4:1, 3), by Pharisees and Sadducees (16:1), and by "some Pharisees" (19:3).

73. And in Mark's parallel account, that author doesn't frame the question as a test.

74. Burge, "Commandment," 151. Burge cites Mishnah Avot 2:1 as an example in this regard.

moral speculation . . . is that it creates an ethical hierarchy weighing the slightest details of religious behavior."[75] And, in Matthew, we have already witnessed Jesus addressing this kind of problem of prioritization head-on. Speaking to scribes and Pharisees, Jesus has warned, "For you tithe mint, dill, and cumin, but you neglect the weightier matters of the law: justice and mercy and loyalty. These you should have done, without neglecting the others" (23:23). So, while the question appears less threatening than the previous two tests, these Pharisees apparently are hoping that Jesus' answer will show him to be idiosyncratic enough to raise suspicions about his interpretation of the Torah.

Jesus answers by bringing together two Torah commands: love God and love neighbor (citing Deut. 6:5 and Lev. 19:18, respectively). Then he concludes, "On these two commandments hang the entire law and the prophets" (22:40). None of the language or the ideas Jesus expresses are unique within his Jewish context.[76] In this way, Jesus aligns himself with the Hebrew Scriptures and faithful interpretation of them.[77] His hermeneutic, centered on love of God and neighbor, is no threat to his faith or to his people. But his hermeneutic does call for a singular loyalty to Israel's God that makes a "claim on the whole person."[78]

75. Burge, "Commandment," 151.

76. John Nolland does suggest that the inclusion of the prophets along with the Torah as "represented by the . . . fundamental principle" of love is distinctive (*Matthew*, 913).

77. As Davies and Allison sum up the teaching of the Matthean Jesus in 22:34–40, "Matthew's text, in other words, postulates that the Torah is in harmony with itself: its twin commandments, to love God and neighbour, are at one with its other commandments; and the suspension of the law and prophets on the commandments to love simply means that all imperatives are to be performed for the sake of God and neighbour" (*Matthew*, 3:246).

78. Nolland, *Matthew*, 908. In contrast to the two previous encounters, Matthew narrates no response by the leaders or the crowds to Jesus' words (22:22, 33). Nolland suggests that the silence of Jesus' opponents that comes from his final words in 22:41–46 may be intended to be "read in" here as well. "Since an outcome is marked (vv. 22, 33, 46) for three of the four question-and-answer scenes and the scene lacking an outcome includes interaction with same gathered Pharisees in the final scene, v. 46 may be intended to mark the outcome of the double scene" (917).

### MATTHEW 22:41–46: THE FINAL RIPOSTE AND RIDDLE

In the final episode of this riddling session initiated by the Jerusalem leaders, Matthew shows Jesus having the last word. And his final word is a riddle. "They had been throwing riddles at him all day; now it was their turn to answer one."[79] Of all the riddles I have proposed in this section of Matthew, this one is by far the most agreed-upon riddle (it is in fact the most agreed-upon riddle in the Synoptic Gospels).[80]

Jesus begins this final confrontation with this question: "What do you think . . . ?" (*ti hymin dokei* [22:42]). We have already noted that this question can signal that a riddle is coming.[81] Jesus' riddle centers on the identity of the Messiah: "What do you think about the Messiah? Whose son is he?" The Pharisees answer that the Messiah is David's son (22:42), an answer that is accurate as far as it goes, and which fits Matthew's "son of David" Christology (1:1; 9:27; 12:23; 15:22; 20:30–31; 21:9, 15).

Jesus confounds that straightforward answer, however, with a riddle constructed from Psalm 110:1:

> How does David by the Spirit call him "Lord," when he says:
> "The Lord said to my Lord,
> 'Sit at my right hand
> until I put your enemies
> under your feet'"?
> So if David calls him "Lord," how can he be his son?
> (22:43–45)

79. Reeves, *Matthew*, 442.

80. With over a half dozen Matthean commentators mentioning explicitly that this is a riddle—e.g., Davies and Allison, *Matthew*, 3:252, 254; Reeves, *Matthew*, 442–43; Mitch and Sri, *Matthew*, 289, 291; Witherington, *Matthew*, 406, 420; Brown and Roberts, *Matthew*, 204–5; Thatcher, *Jesus the Riddler*, 32. Some examples of the many scholars who identify a riddle in Matthew's close parallel in Mark 12:35–37 include Caneday, "Parables and Riddles," 65; Strauss, *Mark*, 548; Novenson, *Grammar of Messianism*, 16; Marshall, *New Testament Theology*, 82.

81. Thatcher, *Jesus the Riddler*, 40–41.

That last question is the heart of the riddle: "If David calls him 'Lord,' how can he be [David's] son?" (22:45). The right answer to this riddle is to avoid choosing one identity over the other. The answer is that the Messiah standing in front of them is both "son of David" and Lord of David. As Rodney Reeves puts it, "Jesus [is] the answer to the riddle."[82] The lordship of Jesus has been hinted at in Matthew already—by Jesus himself (7:21–22; 12:8; 21:3) and by others (e.g., 8:2, 6, 8, 21; 20:30–33). Here it is made clear through the psalm reference that his lordship is tied to his exaltation by God to ultimate kingship[83]—a reality that will be affirmed at the conclusion of Matthew in Jesus' claim to possess "all authority in heaven and on earth" (28:18).

The riddle that Jesus speaks provides a cryptic answer to the question that began the riddling session at 21:23: "By what authority are you doing these things?" The answer: Jesus is "Messiah and Lord"—authorized by Israel's God in all he does.[84] Israel's leaders, who have assumed that they started the riddling session with the upper hand, are now unable to respond. As the final verse of chapter 22 makes clear, "No one was able to say a word in answer to his question. And from that day on, no one dared to question him any longer" (22:46). Jesus' wisdom, employed through questions, riddles, and even evasive tactics when his neck is on the line, quashes his opponents in the end, leaving them speechless.[85]

To sum up, Matthew 21:23–22:46 is a riddling session. I've suggested this genre identification by the sheer number of statements and questions that foster intentional ambiguity. We have also seen confirmation of riddles across these two chapters and through a variety of means: (1) clues from the narrator, including

82. Reeves, *Matthew*, 443.

83. Davies and Allison, *Matthew*, 3:254.

84. Brown and Roberts, *Matthew*, 205.

85. Garland provides this summary: "The expert Jewish teachers have not only been unable to prevail over [Jesus] in verbal jousts, they are reduced to an embarrassing silence, unable to interpret the Scripture. Jesus stands . . . as the authoritative interpreter" (*Reading Matthew*, 226).

the mentioning of traps and tests; (2) clues from the various characters as they ask ambiguous questions of Jesus and Jesus responds with his own questions; and (3) responses from the various character audiences, including utter amazement from both crowds and leaders and, in the final turn, absolute silence.

## The Interpretive Significance of Riddles in Matthew

We now turn to the question of the difference it makes to identify riddles in Matthew. Once we have noticed the presence of riddles and even an entire riddling session, what should that do for our interpretive practices as we read and study Matthew? First, we will consider the hermeneutical significance of riddles for understanding the teachings of Jesus, and then we will reflect on the importance of riddles for understanding Jesus himself.

### *The (at Times) Ambiguous Quality of Jesus' Teachings*

The first interpretive implication of the regular presence of riddles in Matthew is that we should adjust our assumptions about how transparent Jesus is at any turn. If riddles are, by definition, intentionally ambiguous, then Jesus, if we grant that he used riddles, was not always fully transparent as he taught. At times, Jesus intended to be ambiguous.

It bears repeating that this does not mean that there is a riddle under every Matthean rock. Riddles are most effective when employed for particular purposes in specific contexts. And plenty of Jesus' teachings in Matthew are *unambiguous* in their meaning. Consider Matthew 5:44, where Jesus exhorts his followers, "Love your enemies and pray for those who persecute you." What Jesus expects might be difficult to live out, but it is not particularly difficult to understand.

If Jesus' teachings were sometimes intentionally ambiguous, however, readers of Matthew will want to be attentive to the multiple possible referents embedded in a riddle. We will want to shift our genre expectation as we encounter these riddles. When we come upon what looks to be a riddle by the criteria already outlined, a first move would be to *slow down our reading and shift our interpretive frame to acknowledge and press into the ambiguity*. Knowing that multiple referents are likely within a riddle, we can sketch out the various possibilities and consider which referent might be in view. And we'll want to realize that the most obvious answer may not be the one intended. We should also be careful to think beyond binaries that riddles sometimes set up and that they often mean to interrogate. Ben Witherington highlights the need for such a thoughtful reading strategy: "Wisdom literature requires patience and time. Since so much of Wisdom literature involves indirect speech (metaphors, similes, figures, images, and riddles) rather than straight-forward propositions or normal discourse, one is obliged not merely to read the Wisdom material but also to ruminate upon it."[86]

Hermeneutically, riddles require rumination. They invite us to ponder longer than might be expected. We can illustrate the invitation to ruminate by returning to Jesus' riddle about paying the imperial tax. Jesus answers the question about paying the tax by suggesting a binary between what belongs to Caesar and what belongs to God. The riddle allows for either answer (to pay or not to pay), depending on what the hearer puts in each category. Initially, hearers could assume that if the coin belongs to Caesar, then it should be returned to him (the imperial tax should be paid). But what about the inscription on the coin that Jesus has called attention to—the one that claims for Caesar not just all political authority but also all-encompassing religious authority? Does such wide-ranging authority really belong to Caesar? Or does all authority belong exclusively to Israel's God, who owns and rules over all things? This ambiguity allows Jesus to evade the

86. Witherington, *Jesus the Sage*, 3.

trap set for him. But Matthew's audience is meant to sit with the riddle and ruminate. They are invited to ponder these ambiguities long enough to hear the riddle's implicit exhortation to full allegiance to the one true God. As Warren Carter suggests, this saying of Jesus "establishes loyalty to God and God's purposes as the ultimate loyalty."[87]

Let's try out this strategy of lingering and ruminating on another potential Matthean riddle. Jesus twice gives the following aphorism to his disciples: "Whoever finds their life will lose it, and whoever loses their life for me will find it" (10:39 [cf. similar language at 16:25]). W. D. Davies and Dale Allison, in their commentary, suggest that this could well be a riddle.[88] It does fit the definition of a riddle, in that its referents are ambiguous. Between the first and second lines, Jesus uses "finds" (*heuriskō*) and "loses" (*apollymi*) in two different ways. He also employs "life" (*psychē*) with two distinct meanings: *psychē* can be one's present, temporal existence or one's eschatological, eternal existence with God.[89] The riddle plays on these single words to mean more than one thing in close context. Such wordplays create ambiguity and invite rumination. Upon reflection, to "find one's life" in the first clause has to do with attempts to "find life" on one's own, apart from Jesus. But "finding life" in the second clause is granted because of losing one's life for Jesus. "True 'life' is not what human beings acquire for themselves, but what God will grant them precisely through *death*." The riddle functions as a "promise for those who for Jesus' sake surrender their life."[90] There is a deep paradox here.[91]

Yet the paradox that sits at the center of this saying—this riddle—can be masked by our sheer familiarity with it. Many of

87. Carter, *Matthew and the Margins*, 440.

88. Davies and Allison explain its authenticity based on its multiple attestation and the reality that "Jesus was fond of riddles or paradoxes" (*Matthew*, 2:223). Witherington also notes the possibility that 10:39 is a riddle (*Jesus the Sage*, 172).

89. BDAG, 1099.

90. Luz, *Matthew 8–20*, 116.

91. France refers to 10:39 as a "paradoxical epigram" (*Matthew*, 411).

us are so closely acquainted with this teaching and many other sayings of Jesus that we have potentially normalized them to sound self-evident. It can help our hermeneutical approach to consider how such riddles would have landed on the ears of the first hearers of Jesus (the story audience), who may have been more than a little befuddled by his wordplays about life and death at a point in his ministry where it was far from clear that his messianic mission would reach its zenith on a Roman cross.[92]

With all this conversation about ambiguity, I offer an important caveat. The presence of riddles across Jesus' teachings is *not* an argument for a Gnostic portrait of Jesus and his teachings. The teachings of Jesus aren't aimed at a chosen few and obscure to all the rest, a view that later Gnostic writers would promote.[93] Instead, in the Gospels and in Matthew specifically, the invitation from Jesus to listen and understand is a real one, even if it points to the need for open and receptive listening and continued rumination for understanding to occur. As Jesus reiterates, "The one who has ears ought to listen" (11:15; 13:9, 43).[94]

What we can say about at least some of Jesus' teachings in the Gospels, and in Matthew particularly, is that they confound before they illuminate. And they often confound the disciples who follow Jesus as well as his opponents (e.g., 15:1–20). Yet Matthew expects that his audience—believers who know and understand Jesus to be the crucified and risen Messiah—will understand Jesus' teachings as he communicates them, riddles and all. In fact, those who struggle to understand what Jesus is saying at any particular

92. Sometimes, as we have seen, Matthew makes clear the confusion of the audience on the story level (22:22, 33, 46). Other examples of ambiguous sayings that have been identified as riddles in Matthew's Gospel include 11:11 (Stein, *Method and Message*, 18); 11:12, 14 (Thatcher, *Jesus the Riddler*, 32); 24:28 (Stein, *Method and Message*, 18).

93. Often, in these Gnostic writings, even Jesus' "inner circle" cannot understand his teachings—e.g., the Gospel of Judas, where no one other than Judas understands Jesus' teachings.

94. Brown, "Rhetoric of Hearing," 266–67. As I explore in this essay, the Matthean invitation to listen and understand is borrowed from Isaiah.

part of the story line function as a foil for Matthew's readers, who are meant to comprehend what the storied characters often struggle to understand.[95]

This observation about Matthean readers aligns with the bidirectional influence of an embedded genre with its macrogenre—a hermeneutical concept introduced in chapter 1. There, I suggested a dialectic relationship between the overarching genre and its embedded genre, in which each genre impacts the other. In the present chapter, we have focused on how riddles are used in a Gospel, so our attention has landed on how the embedded genre of riddle has impacted the macrogenre of narrative or biography. But what about the influence of the narrative on the riddles used in it? Are there interpretive insights to be gained from considering how Matthew's narrative genre impacts embedded riddles?

I suggest that the hermeneutical impact of bringing a riddle into a narrative story line is potentially to make it *less riddle-like*. In some instances, Matthew's narrative disambiguates a riddle, especially if we keep in mind the distinction between what Matthean characters understand and what the Matthean audience is meant to comprehend.

We can explore this distinction and effect by looking at another riddle in Matthew: the Jonah riddle. In Matthew 12, certain Pharisees and scribes come to Jesus and demand a sign (*sēmeion* [12:38]). Jesus expressly indicates that they will receive no sign, "except the sign of Jonah the prophet" (12:39). This language of *no sign except this sign* already hints that the "sign" they will receive is not much of a sign at all (at least, not a miraculous sign).[96] Instead, it might be a riddle. The "sign of Jonah" (*to sēmeion Iōna*) is ambiguous, and intentionally so, I suggest. Its referent

95. For example, the disciples often function as a foil for Matthew's implied or ideal reader. See Brown, *Disciples*, 130.

96. As Luz notes, *sēmeion* is never used for "miracle" in the Synoptics (*Matthew 8–20*, 216).

is decidedly ambiguous. What part of the Jonah story from the Jewish Scriptures is evoked with this language? Is it Nineveh's repentance, or Jonah's rescue from the fish, or both? Or something else? As I note elsewhere, "Jesus refuses to pander to their demand [for a sign]. . . . Instead of the sign they desire, Jesus gives them a riddle about his destiny."[97]

If Jesus is riddling in his reference to "the sign of Jonah," then his subsequent words might at least provide a partial explanation of the riddle: "For as Jonah was in the belly of the sea creature for three days and three nights, so the Son of Man will be in the heart of the earth for three days and three nights" (12:40). Jesus implies that it is God's rescue of Jonah from the fish after three days and nights that provides the meaning of the riddle.[98] It is interesting that Luke's parallel to this Matthean passage offers a more clipped "explanation."

> As the crowds increased, Jesus said, "This is a wicked generation. It asks for a sign, but none will be given it except the sign of Jonah. For as Jonah was a sign to the Ninevites, so also will the Son of Man be to this generation." (Luke 11:29–30)

Matthew's version disambiguates the "riddle of Jonah" more than Luke's does. Yet even the explanation provided by Jesus in Matthew 12:40 has a measure of ambiguity: *Who is the Son of Man Jesus refers to?*[99] *And what does it mean that this one will be in the heart of the earth?* At this stage in the narrative its characters are not likely to understand the riddle or its partial explanation.

97. Brown and Roberts, *Matthew*, 125. Schnackenburg identifies the "sign of Jonah" as a riddle (*Matthew*, 118). See also Jeremias, "Ἰωνᾶς," *TDNT*, 3:410. Luz acknowledges its riddle-like quality but argues against this designation because of its purported function as a "sign" (*Matthew 8–20*, 215).

98. Even as Jesus highlights the differing responses of the present generation and "the citizens of Nineveh" from the Jonah narrative.

99. The referent "Son of Man" is used by Jesus across the narrative for himself but not always clearly so for the story audience (i.e., it seems to be used purposefully with some amount of ambiguity).

Yet Matthew does not leave this riddle behind. Toward the end of Jesus' Galilean ministry, Pharisees and Sadducees come to him and ask for "a sign from heaven" (16:1). Matthew signals in this case that these leaders are testing him with their request, providing a clue from the narrator that Jesus might respond with a riddle. As he has done earlier, Jesus refuses their request and critiques those who need a sign but are unable to interpret what is right in front of them—that is, Jesus himself and the many miracles he has done. Jesus again refers to "the sign of Jonah" as the only "sign" that will be given (16:4).[100]

While on the story level of Matthew no characters appear to understand Jesus' riddle, on Matthew's discourse level the implied reader is very likely expected to comprehend this riddle of Jonah. At least by the time the implied reader arrives at 16:21, they will hear Jesus refer to his coming death and to his resurrection "on the third day" (also at 17:23; 20:19). The reference to Jonah's three days and nights (12:40) is clarified sufficiently to hear the answer to the riddle. Matthew's narrative context (the macrogenre) has shed light on this riddle Jesus gives.

### *Jesus as Expert Riddler in Matthew: Christological Implications*

To conclude this exploration of riddles in Matthew, we turn to consider the christological implications of the Matthean Jesus as one who tells riddles, and tells them with some frequency. We can begin with Ben Witherington's observation that riddles, along with other teaching forms, were handed down within the early church, at least in part because they were believed to *say something about Jesus.*[101]

Framed this way, what does Matthew say about this Jesus who sometimes speaks in riddles? First, the ability of Jesus to outwit

100. And Jesus provides no explanation at all of the riddle or sign, as he had at 12:40.
101. Witherington, *Jesus the Sage*, 204.

leaders who confront him and try to trap him shows that he is wise beyond all others. While Matthew affirms many roles for Jesus—prophet, teacher, and Messiah, to name just a few—he also accents *Jesus as sage*. Matthew does so mostly implicitly, through Jesus' capacity to evade the traps set for him by giving a wise response (or deferral of a response). He astounds those listening to him by his wisdom. For example, people of his own hometown wonder aloud about the source of his wisdom: "Where did this one gain such wisdom and the power to do miracles?" (13:54). We also see Jesus as sage in his extensive teaching in Matthew's Gospel that draws from the Jewish Scriptures, in both form and content, and announces and explains the arriving reign of God.[102]

Yet Matthew not only casts Jesus as the wisest of teachers; he also implies that Jesus is the very embodiment of Wisdom.[103] In Matthew 11:2–30, the evangelist implicitly but clearly indicates that Jesus should be understood as Wisdom. First, he frames 11:2–19 with an *inclusio*, aligning the Messiah's "deeds" (11:2: *ta erga*) with Wisdom's "deeds" (11:19: *ta erga*). Additionally, at the end of Matthew 11, Jesus offers an invitation that sounds very much like Wisdom's invitation in Proverbs and other Jewish wisdom books, such as Sirach. Matthew's Jesus invites, "Come to me, all who are weary and weighed down, and I will give you rest. Take my yoke upon you and learn from me, for I am lowly and humble in heart, and you will find rest for your souls. For my yoke is easy and my load is light" (11:28–30).[104] Given this *inclusio*

102. As Witherington notes, Jesus "casts his teaching in a recognizably sapiential form" (e.g., riddles) (*Jesus the Sage*, 159).

103. Matthew prepares the way for this christological category by showing in the Sermon on the Mount that Jesus is the authoritative teacher of the Torah (5:17–48; 7:28–29), with Torah and Wisdom sharing significant conceptual space within first-century Judaism.

104. Note, for example, the similarities with Sir. 51:26–27: "'Put your neck under her *yoke*, and let your *souls* receive instruction; it is to be found close by.' See with your own eyes that I have *labored* but little and *found* for myself much *serenity*" (NRSVue). For the terms shared between the LXX of Sir. 51:26–27 and Matt. 11:28–30 (which are italicized here), see Brown and Roberts, *Matthew*, 117.

and these Wisdom echoes, when Jesus invites the weary to come to him, "it is God's Wisdom speaking."[105]

This chapter began by considering this question: "Does Matthew portray Jesus as a Messiah who riddles?" I've answered that question in the affirmative, showing how Jesus in Matthew outwits and sometimes confounds his opponents, and even confuses his followers at times, as he expresses divine wisdom. *Jesus is the wisest of all teachers.* Yet Matthew doesn't stop there. He shows Jesus as riddler to demonstrate that Jesus is the very embodiment of divine Wisdom. God's ways are not always immediately discernible because they do not follow the same path as human wisdom. So, Matthew's Jesus invites those who would follow him to listen intently to his words: "The one who has ears ought to listen" (11:15). And this Jesus invites all who would follow him to learn from him (11:29). For Matthew's reader, the invitation is to follow Messiah Jesus, who is *Wisdom in the flesh.*

105. Brown and Roberts, *Matthew*, 389. In Matt. 11, the theme of wisdom is highlighted as well by the rejection motif of 11:20–24 and riddles and questions clustered in 11:11–15.

FOUR

# Why Put a Household Code in the Middle of a Letter?

## *The* Haustafel *in 1 Peter*

Even if you've never seen the TV show *Father Knows Best*, a Hollywood sitcom from the 1950s,[1] the title communicates volumes about cultural values and norms prevalent during that era. The show's characterizations of its nuclear family—father, mother, two daughters, and a son—promoted what were considered at the time normal roles for parents and children, males and females.[2] These kinds of norms would also have been reflected and enforced in the legal structures and civic discourse of

1. Based on the radio show of the same title from the early 1950s.

2. Even as some of the episodes pressed the envelope in terms of cultural roles related to gender. See season 2, episode 30: "Betty, Girl Engineer" (https://www.youtube.com/watch?v=sGxHDK_D0UE).

that era. Everything from tax exemptions and laws that impacted marriage, to literature and education, to religious communities (and, as we've noted, Hollywood) would have both shaped and reflected cultural norms.

My primary point in raising these examples from my own United States context is to indicate how norms and expectations for family life, and even definitions of family, are "in the air" in any particular epoch. We may not be actively aware of every avenue for pressures to conform to an "ideal family" and to perform the roles of "ideal family members," but if we have lived in a specific context and era, we know, and we know implicitly, what is expected of us in our family functions.

As we look at our final "genre within a genre," we turn to the Letter of 1 Peter. Within this letter, we encounter a "household code." Household or domestic codes in the Greco-Roman world were an important means of casting a vision for the "ideal family" and pressing members of society toward conformity with that vision. These written norms were not exactly like the TV show *Father Knows Best*, but, possibly surprisingly, they share in common with that show some general purposes and functions.

## The Prominence and Purpose of the Household Code in 1 Peter

The Letter of 1 Peter is five chapters long—105 verses. And twenty-seven of these verses are devoted to a *household code* (2:11–3:12). That means that a full quarter of 1 Peter consists of this domestic code. Even more striking, the household code comes pretty much at the center point of 1 Peter.[3] Leonhard Goppelt identifies the core section that includes the household code (2:11–4:11) as "the center and focus of the letter."[4]

3. By counting verses, we see that it arrives thirty-five verses into the letter (with forty-three verses following it).

4. Goppelt, *I Peter*, 20.

If you're writing a letter to the Christians of Asia Minor or Anatolia (modern-day Turkey or Türkiye) in the first century, why put a household code at the heart of your dispatch? That's a question that has engaged me for years, and it is the question addressed in this chapter. Answering that question involves getting to know what a "household code" in the world of the first century looked like. And it means diving into issues of who these early Christians were and what in their situation and experiences pressed the author of 1 Peter to include and adapt a household code *as a key strategy* for his epistle.[5]

To begin, we will need to get a general sense of the function of household or domestic codes in the Greco-Roman world. Why, generally speaking, does someone write or recite a domestic code? A domestic code communicates societal norms for ordering the household and the behavior expected of the individuals that make up the household. A domestic code, generally speaking, encourages compliance with these expected societal norms. The intended function of a household code, in a nutshell, is *conformity*. This is true of domestic codes in the Greco-Roman world of the first century as much as it is true of modern "codes" that we see implicitly woven into the carriers of such norms, such as the media and civic discourse.

Having mentioned the conforming function of the ancient household code, I can back up and ask why the audience of 1 Peter might have needed such a code, at least from the perspective of the author of the letter. Why might he have considered it necessary for Christians in Anatolia to hear and engage a household code?

### *Who Needs to Hear a Household Code?*

To begin to answer this question, we can analyze the situation of the audience of 1 Peter, especially as we can glean it from the

5. Although there is significant debate over the authorship of 1 Peter, my historical arguments related to ancient household codes do not depend on any precise dating of the letter (60s if Petrine authorship is genuine; 80s–90s if otherwise).

letter itself. We begin with the clues drawn from 1 Peter 4:3–4, a text that illuminates this situation quite well.

> For you have already spent enough time acting as the gentiles like to act—living in excess, evil cravings, drunkenness, reveling, carousing, and in disgusting idolatry. They are astonished that you are no longer joining them in that same flood of reckless abandon, so they malign you.[6]

In this short description, two things become clear. First, the audience of the letter is primarily (though likely not completely) gentile—an amorphous group that would include people from a variety of ethnicities and past religious loyalties. We see this in the description of their former lifestyle, which was characterized by idolatry and all the problematic behaviors that Jewish people associated with worshiping pagan gods in pagan temples.[7] A nod to the gentile identity of the letter's audience has already been offered earlier in the letter, where they are steered away from "your evil desires when you formerly were in ignorance" (1:14) and where Peter has described their salvation as a redemption "from your useless way of life you inherited from your ancestors" (1:18; cf. 2:10).[8]

A second reality of the letter's audience is illuminated in the verses from chapter 4 quoted above. This group of Christians is being verbally harassed because they have disassociated themselves from temple activities performed for their former

6. All translations of 1 Peter are my own from my forthcoming commentary, unless otherwise indicated (Brown, *1 Peter*, forthcoming).

7. It is no accident that the list concludes with the climactic "disgusting idolatry," as Jewish and Christian writers frequently associated the other activities in the list with the worship of (false) gods (i.e., idols). Such writers often associated idolatry with a catalog of vices (and as the source of vice). See, for example, Wis. 14:8–14 (and note other sources referenced in Achtemeier, *1 Peter*, 281n74).

8. At two points in the letter the author disassociates his primarily gentile audience from their gentile communities by referring to nonbelievers as "gentiles" (2:12; 4:3).

gods. As Travis Williams proposes, 1 Peter 4:3–4 "reveals that prior to their conversion some members of the audience had been involved in certain social activities or institutions, and upon conversion they were no longer able to continue in these practices."[9] Their neighbors, friends, and, as we'll discover, even some *within their own household* are surprised by their withdrawal from these socioreligious activities. As a result, these other people—still committed to their gods—"malign" or verbally slander the Petrine Christians, who have turned their backs on the gods. This glimpse into the kind of mistreatment the letter's recipients are experiencing is confirmed repeatedly across 1 Peter:

- "Make sure your conduct is honorable among the gentiles, so that, *when they accuse you of doing what is wrong*, they might see your good deeds and glorify God in the day of his visitation" (2:12).
- "For it is God's will for your community that, by doing good, you should *silence the uninformed words of ignorant people*" (2:15).
- "Do not repay evil with evil or *slander* with *slander*" (3:9).
- "If you are *reviled* for Christ's name, you are actually blessed" (4:14).[10]

To gain an appreciation for the cost of withdrawing from temple expectations and activities, we need to understand the values and sensibilities of Greco-Roman religion and society in the first-century world (and in Anatolia specifically). The Greco-Roman pantheon, as well as locally specific, ancestral deities and the Roman imperial cult, would have populated the religious

9. Williams, *Persecution in 1 Peter*, 241.

10. See also 2:22–23 for the example of Jesus and his nonretaliatory stance when he suffered insults.

landscape. "In such a setting, civic and religious expectations promoted loyalty to and worship of multiple deities, even if someone might maintain a preference or special connection to one particular god. What was little understood or accepted was allegiance to only one god (and that one not recognized as part of the Greek or Roman pantheon), as promoted by those who worshipped Messiah Jesus exclusively. When Christians proclaimed Christ and Christ alone as Lord, they were rejecting a primary religious and civic duty."[11]

Although temples provided a centralized location for cultic activity, temple influence and related expectations for religious and social life had a much broader impact. As Williams enumerates, cultic influence impacted everyday life through such varied means as (trade) guilds and associations (which often were closely aligned with worship of the gods), public buildings and institutions (e.g., with their inscriptions to the gods and/or the imperial family), festivals and games, and other public rituals.[12]

Separation from these many and various activities would have attracted attention and would have labeled Christians as "antisocial," with the fallout being potentially economic and political as well as religious.[13] In such a situation, Christians were susceptible "to charges of wrongdoing and conduct injurious to the well-being of the commonwealth and the favor of the gods."[14]

We can hear the difficulties arising from this scenario in 1 Peter 3:14–16, where the author writes,

> Do not be afraid of them; do not be unsettled. But set apart Christ as Lord in your lives, being ready at every turn to give an answer

11. Brown (*Philippians*, 50) describes the religious terrain of first-century Philippi, but this is applicable to first-century Anatolia as well (see Williams, *Persecution in 1 Peter*, 245–55).

12. Williams, *Persecution in 1 Peter*, 245–55.

13. We can see this reality described in narrative form in Acts 16:19–24; 19:24–27.

14. Elliott, *1 Peter*, 94.

> to everyone who asks you for the reason for your common hope. But do so considerately and respectfully, keeping your conscience clear, so that, when you are maligned, those who disparage your good conduct in Christ may be put to shame. (3:14b–16)

Setting apart Christ as Lord in their lives[15] would necessitate a rejection of the lordship of others gods (cf. 1 Cor. 8:5–6) and would have placed these Christians in a precarious situation—one that seems to have caused them to fear for their own well-being (3:14) as they bore the brunt of malicious slander (3:16). The exclusivity of Christian worship was, in effect, a "denial of the gods."[16] Williams suggests that "failure to worship the [traditional] gods bore certain implications for members of the entire community [i.e., the entire populace]. If one member slighted the gods, it was believed, retribution could have been exacted upon everyone."[17]

So how, specifically, does a household code help this group of beleaguered Christians? The Petrine household code helps these Christians to walk the fine line between accommodation to cultural norms as much as possible and resistance to some societal expectations when absolutely necessary. If a household code typically presses for conformity, this particular household code, especially in its unusual features, also implicitly affirms the singular loyalty due to Christ that inevitably has placed these Petrine believers in a difficult and potentially dangerous situation.

And Peter gives them a household code, not least because the dividing line of allegiance seems to be running right down the middle of some of these Anatolian households. This reality becomes clear as Peter directly addresses slaves whose masters are

15. The phrase *kyrion de ton Christon hagiasate en tais kardiais hymōn* (3:15) speaks to the singular loyalty that Christians are to prioritize at the center of their entire life (for *kardia* as the center of one's entire life, see BDAG, 508).

16. Williams's phrase (*Persecution in 1 Peter*, 255).

17. Williams, *Persecution in 1 Peter*, 257.

harsh (not just the tolerant ones) (2:18) and wives whose husbands are not believers (3:1). As we will see, this puts these slaves and women who have "set apart" Christ as Lord as the object of their singular loyalty in a potentially perilous position in their homes.

### *A Look at Ancient Domestic Codes*

We can look all the way back to Plato (428–347 BCE) to illuminate the genre of the household code.[18] An important connection that Plato makes involves an integral relationship between the household and the state (Greek, *polis*). Plato proposes that the household and the *polis* are "organised under the same principle of rule."[19] For example, Plato refers to "the matter of ruling and being ruled, alike in the [s]tates, large or small, and in households."[20] Later, Plato distinguishes between those who rule and those who are ruled: "The better are the superiors of the worse, and the older in general of the younger; [t]herefore also parents are superior to their offspring, men to women and children, rulers to ruled."[21]

Aristotle (384–322 BCE), a student of Plato, focuses on the relational pairings that form the core of the household: "master and slave, husband and wife, father and children."[22] You may have noticed that the ancient household is described in different terms than is the household as conceived in contemporary Western societies. Not only would the ancient household have included a wider array of groups, which could include multiple family generations and, as noted by Aristotle, slaves,[23] but also it often functioned

18. Although the topos of "household management" was not original to Plato (see Balch, *Let Wives Be Submissive*, 25).

19. E.g., *Laws* 3.689e–690c. See Hering, *Colossian and Ephesian* Haustafeln, 205.

20. *Laws* 3.690a (Bury, LCL).

21. *Laws* 11.917a (Bury, LCL).

22. *Politics* 1.2.1, 1253b (Rackham, LCL).

23. Caroline Johnson Hodge also mentions the possible presence of teachers, nurses, and staff to help in fields or shops ("'Holy Wives,'" 4).

as a locus of economic activity. Unsurprisingly, Aristotle sometimes wove into his three relational pairs an additional economic category related to household wealth.

The three pairs that Aristotle references in his *Politics* should sound familiar to readers of the New Testament, given the framing of the two domestic codes in Ephesians and Colossians, both of which include these three pairings of "master and slave, husband and wife, father and children" (cf. Eph. 5:21–6:9; Col. 3:18–4:1).[24] Aristotle writes elsewhere in his *Politics*, "It is a part of the household science to rule over wife and children."[25] Notice that this address is framed for the male head of household. This is an important feature of the Greek (and Roman) domestic codes: In most cases, guidance and norms are addressed and given to the one who rules. The male head was expected to exercise authority over his wife, his children, and his slaves (albeit in ways distinctive to the particular relationship).[26]

Since Plato and Aristotle lived and wrote hundreds of years before the New Testament era, it is fair to ask if we could expect the household guidance provided by these philosophers to still have purchase by the time of the writing of 1 Peter. David Balch, in his seminal work on the Petrine household code, has shown that both Plato and Aristotle came to be read and cited in the decades leading up to the first century CE, most likely through the influence of handbooks that contained salient portions of

24. The ordering is not identical to Aristotle's formulation, but the three pairs appear in both Ephesians and Colossians. For the argument that the Ephesian household code "is far less accommodating to [Roman ideology] than has often been recognized," see Winzenburg, *Ephesians and Empire*, 234.

25. *Politics* 1.5.1, 1259a (Rackham, LCL). He goes on: "For the male is by nature better fitted to command than the female" (*Politics* 1.5.1, 1259a).

26. Johnson Hodge notes that the head of the house usually, though not always, was male and gives Lydia in Acts 16 as a counterexample ("'Holy Wives,'" 2). Nijay Gupta addresses Nympha (Col. 4:15) as an example of a woman who stepped into the role of head of household (potentially as a widow) and so served as *materfamilias* within her household (*Tell Her Story*, 190–92).

those earlier writings.[27] This recirculation of the work of Plato and Aristotle focused on, among other things, their discussions of household management, which involved the governing of relationships within the household and the philosophical rationale for such ordering.[28] Balch highlights the Roman writers Dionysius of Halicarnassus, Areius Didymus, and Seneca (each of whom wrote sometime within the first century BCE or CE) to show that "the kind of ethic found in the NT household codes was important to the Roman aristocracy."[29]

We can also trace the influence of the genre of household code on Jewish writers such as Philo and Josephus, who lived and wrote during the first century of the Common Era. Both express the traditional, hierarchical view of the relationship between husbands and wives. For example, Josephus, pointing to the Torah, argues, "Let [the wife] accordingly be submissive, not for her humiliation, but that she may be directed; for the authority has been given by God to the man."[30] Philo expresses similar sentiments and actually uses the language of "servitude" for a wife's stance toward her husband.[31] We can set this response in context

27. Balch, *Let Wives Be Submissive*, 37–38.

28. Balch writes, "Unquestionably the closest parallels to the texts quoted above from Seneca, Hierocles, Philo, and Josephus are found in Plato and Aristotle, though in authors of the first and second centuries A.D., these ideas almost certainly were mediated through a handbook similar to that of Areius Didymus" (*Let Wives Be Submissive*, 55–56).

29. Balch, *Let Wives Be Submissive*, 74. He notes that this is precisely "the class from which governors for the provinces was drawn" (e.g., those mentioned in 1 Pet. 2:14). As Balch summarizes the influence of Aristotle on first-century writers, "Aristotelian political ideas were preserved by the Periapatetics. They were outlined in detail by the Stoic Areius Didymus in a popular handbook perhaps intended for Augustus Caesar. They were discussed at length, and rejected, by the Epicurean Philodemus. Elements of the topos were known to the Roman Cicero and to the Hellenistic Jew Philo" (*Let Wives Be Submissive*, 117). He further delineates later writers who were reliant on Aristotle's threefold outline on this topic (117).

30. *Against Apion* 2.200–201 (Thackeray, LCL).

31. *Hypothetica* 7.3: "Wives must be in servitude [*douleuō*] to the husbands." According to James Hering, Philo's call to "servitude" here is unique in the household literature more generally (*Colossian and Ephesian* Haustafeln, 234).

by noting Roman critiques of Judaism for its destabilizing and even subversive influence. For example, the Roman politician Tacitus describes the Jewish people this way: "The Jews regard as profane all that we [Romans] hold sacred; on the other hand, they permit all that we abhor."[32] As Balch proposes, Josephus and Philo could very well be responding to these kinds of critiques by emphasizing traditional mores and expectations.[33] These Jewish contributions and the setting in which they arise are suggestive for our understanding of the New Testament domestic codes, which can also be understood as responses to external political and social critiques of Christian communities and attendant pressure toward conformity.

Although we have been addressing and noticing the patterns of similarity between classical domestic codes and those of the Roman period, it is important to recognize that not all first-century Greco-Roman writers consistently followed Plato and Aristotle. Some later Greek and Roman writers expressed more egalitarian impulses than were evident in the earlier forms—for example, Plutarch and some Roman Stoic philosophers. Seneca, one such Roman Stoic philosopher (4 BCE–65 CE), suggests a certain kind of reciprocity in the relationships between husband and wife, master and slave, and parent and child,[34] at least in terms of the "equal demand upon both" parties to provide benefit to the other, even if the parties are unequal in status.[35]

Nevertheless, the historical movement is not a simple unidirectional one from hierarchy to egalitarianism. As we might

32. *Histories* 5.4 (Moore, LCL).

33. Balch, *Let Wives Be Submissive*, 73–74. Hering notes, however, that Philo is more progressive regarding slaves, since he views their enslavement as a result of misfortune and not, like Aristotle, because of nature (*Colossian and Ephesian* Haustafeln, 240). Balch issues the important caveat that "it is incorrect to portray [Josephus's and Philo's] 'Jewish' ideas as more repressive than those of Greek thinkers" ("Household Codes," 31).

34. See Balch, *Let Wives Be Submissive*, 51–52.

35. *On Benefits* 2.18.1 (Basore, LCL); cf. 3.18.1–4.

expect, the actual picture is more complex. Even writers, contemporary to the New Testament, who exhibit impulses in the direction of greater equality continue to reflect "the consistent patriarchal pattern seen in Aristotle, Neopythagoreans, *and* in Roman Stoics."[36] Generally, within Greco-Roman philosophy and rhetoric, the male head of the household—in Latin, the *paterfamilias*—had the authority over his wife, children, and slaves, and he was expected to exercise that authority. As these writers reflect on "household management," their writings are intended to promote conformity to these "ideal" hierarchical relations. And while the reality of household relationships would have inevitably been more complex than (male, free) philosophers would admit,[37] the force of the general contours of the ancient domestic code would have routinely shaped expectations and behaviors.[38]

Before turning to the Petrine domestic code, we will find it helpful to return to a distinctive feature of the various discussions of the topic of "household management": the close connection drawn between household and state. Plato highlights this connection, and Aristotle affirms it as well. For these two and for various later writers dependent on them, "good citizenship in the sphere of the household helps to ensure the same in the *polis*."[39] For instance, Gaius Musonius Rufus (ca. 25–ca. 95 CE), a Roman

36. Balch, "Household Codes," 32. He explains, "Roman Stoics were egalitarian in theory but Aristotelian in practice" (31).

37. As Carolyn Osiek and Margaret MacDonald note in their discussion of female roles in early house churches, "Despite the clear reinforcement of the authority of the *paterfamilias* in the household, the authority of the mother in the Lord may often have been a far more present reality for many people" (*A Woman's Place*, 132). And as Bruce Winter has argued, social currents like the phenomenon of the "new" Roman woman, who exercised more freedom in her marriage and social life, could very well have exerted some influence on social ideals and norms, even outside of Italy (*Roman Wives, Roman Widows*).

38. What Osiek and MacDonald refer to as "the complicated relationship between rhetoric and reality" (*A Woman's Place*, 245).

39. Brown, "Just a Busybody?," 567. For example, Hering notes that Musonius Rufus understood "the home in terms of the welfare of the state," though he notes

Stoic, understood "the home in terms of the welfare of society."[40] Musonius insists, "It would be each man's duty to take thought of his own city, and to make of his home a rampart for its [the city's] protection."[41] As we will see, the way the Petrine author begins his household code (2:13–17) suggests that this integral connection between household and state is being assumed for his audience and their context.

## Analyzing the Petrine Household Code

### *Shifting Genre Expectations from Letter to Household Code*

With a clear sense of what ancient household codes often looked like and what their purposes were, we can consider reading strategies for 1 Peter as we move from the overarching genre of letter to the specific subgenre of household code at 2:11 and following. Then we'll explore the Petrine code to see where and how it might fit genre parameters as well as how it bends and expands genre expectations for household codes.

The context preceding the household code in 1 Peter involves some expected elements of the genre of letter, including *exhortations* to the letter's specific audience and *affirmations* for them—in the case of 1 Peter, affirmations of their (new) identity as the people of God. Both exhortations and affirmations are situated in light of the particularly trying circumstances of these Anatolian house churches, as they experience the push and pull of societal forces, some of which are deeply at odds with their newfound allegiance to Jesus as Messiah. After the letter's opening (1:1–12), the author gives a number of initial exhortations to his

that Musonius did not "discuss the household as an economic or political unit" (*Colossian and Ephesian* Haustafeln, 245).

40. Hering, *Colossian and Ephesian* Haustafeln, 245.

41. Musonius, 14.30–34 (Lutz, *Musonius Rufus*, 92–93). Musonius goes on to propose that "the first step toward making his home such a rampart is marriage."

readers to live distinctively within society and in line with their hope in Christ (1:13–2:3).[42] He follows these admonitions with key affirmations about the audience's identity as the people of God, using metaphors connecting their identity to God's temple, a priesthood, and a holy people (2:4–10). This first major section of the epistle leads into the household code (2:11–3:12). Immediately following the code, the author clarifies the audience's situation of being slandered by others for their allegiance to Christ, while also encouraging them to reflect on whether they can ameliorate that slander by living even more concertedly an irreproachable life (3:13–17).

Focusing on the household code itself, we can begin by noticing how the Petrine domestic code aligns closely with the expectations for the genre. First, two of the three paired relationship categories we have noted are represented in 1 Peter: slaves and masters (2:18–25) and wives and husbands (3:1–7). Missing are any instructions for the parent toward children that we observed in Aristotle's three pairings and in Ephesians and Colossians. Second, the calls for slaves and wives to submit to the *paterfamilias* in 1 Peter 2:18 and 3:1 are quite in line with domestic code expectations for the male head of household to exert authority over wives and slaves.[43] Third, the frame of the Petrine household code (2:11–12 and 3:8–12) explicitly highlights the apologetic nature of the code,[44] which is similar to Jewish appropriations of the ancient

42. These exhortations cluster around five imperatives: commands to hope (1:13), be holy (1:15), live reverently or circumspectly (1:17), love God's people (1:22), and crave what will bring salvation (2:2).

43. Although the use of *hypotassō* ("submit") is almost entirely limited (unique) to the New Testament codes. Plutarch is one of two exceptions to this in Greek literature apart from Christian sources for describing wives vis à vis their husbands (*Conjugal Precepts* 33), the other being Callisthenes (*Deeds of Alexander* 1.22.4) (cited in Hering, *Colossian and Ephesian* Haustafeln, 256, 256n141). Hering also notes that the term usually employed is *hypakouō* ("obey").

44. According to Balch, the function of the household code is apologetic, in that it reassures governing authorities that those who have converted "are obedient slaves and wives, just as the culture expected them to be" (*Let Wives Be Submissive*, 109).

household code to demonstrate that Jewish faith was not at odds with Roman authority and expectations. The Petrine code frame commends good conduct and nonretaliation (2:12; 3:9), with the goal of avoiding further conflict with societal norms.

Even as these alignments with ancient household codes are important to notice, they are the "unmarked" features of the household code (in contrast to "marked" or emphatic elements). Since these features align with expectations, they would not have *stood out* to the original audience. Instead, the unmarked features indicate the ways in which the Petrine code mirrors or resembles closely the (anticipated) household code genre. Hermeneutically, it is crucial to pay special attention to any "marked" features of the household code—those that stand out because they defy the normal parameters and expectations of this genre. It is the "marked" features that are especially important interpretively.

One of the marked features of the Petrine code is the extent of direct address to household slaves and to wives. As we have noted, the pattern of the ancient household code was to address the male head of house to guide his rule of the rest of the household members: wife, slaves, children. Less common was the use of direct address to those members with lesser power in the system. And for slaves to be directly addressed was highly unusual.[45] So the direct and lengthy addresses to slaves (eight verses: 2:18–25) and wives (six verses: 3:1–6), with no corresponding words for masters and only a short address to husbands (one verse: 3:7)—these features are unconventional (or "marked").[46]

Additionally, the absence of any address to fathers in relation to their children seems unusual. In fact, Shively Smith calls it a "conspicuous silence in the letter." She suggests that the author of 1 Peter omits this section from his household code and instead locates the child-parent relationship within "the household of

45. Balch, "Household Codes," 47.
46. Smith, *Strangers to Family*, 80.

God" (4:17), in which God is the father of all believers, who together are God's children (1:14, 17). Because of this new reality (this "new birth" [1:3; cf. 23]), those who are loyal to Jesus are siblings together in God's house (2:17; 5:9), with God as their father.[47] These features—direct address to those with less power in the Petrine households and the omission of a section devoted to the parent-child relationship—are marked or atypical features of the household code.

Another unusual feature of the Petrine code is the opening section addressed to all members of the Christian community, exhorting them toward submission to the governing authorities (2:13–17). Yet this rather anomalous first segment of the code taps into the integral connection made in philosophical discourse between state and household (*polis* and *oikos*), and it accents the political tone of the Petrine domestic code. As Greek philosopher Plutarch remarks, "A man . . . ought to have his household well harmonized who is going to harmonize State, Forum, and friends."[48] We could say that this "political" feature of the Petrine code is marked due to its explicit presence at the front of the code.

As we take a more detailed look at the Petrine household code, we will continue to stay attuned to its marked and unmarked features in relation to the Greco-Roman genre of domestic codes.

### *The Parts of the Petrine Household Code*

#### TO ALL PETRINE CHRISTIANS: RELATING TO THE *POLIS* (2:13–17)

We begin with the first segment of the code, 2:13–17, which addresses submission to governing authorities. Given its position

47. Smith, *Strangers to Family*, 80–81. The author might also omit the traditional address to the father regarding his children because he focuses keen attention on the members of the household pairs on the underside of power who still have significant opportunities for agency in their situations. Children, in these contexts, may have had little to no opportunity for the exercise of that agency.

48. *Advice to Bride and Groom*, 43 (Babbitt, LCL).

at the front of the household code proper, the author of 1 Peter locates his domestic code in the context of the political situation and the stance of his Christian audience. This fits the integral connection assumed in the Greco-Roman world between the household and the state, where "insubordination in the one led to insubordination in the other."[49]

> Submit yourselves to every human authority for the Lord's sake, whether to the emperor, as the one who holds the highest place of authority, or to governors, as those who are sent by the emperor to punish wrongdoing and to approve doing good. For it is God's will for your community that, by doing good, you should silence the uninformed words of ignorant people. Live as those who are free, not using your freedom as a guise for evil; instead, live as slaves of God. Honor all people, love the family of believers, fear God, honor the emperor.

What we see in this first section of the code, which is addressed to everyone in the Petrine house churches, is an exhortation to comply with expected norms of submission to the state: "Submit yourselves to every human authority . . . , whether to the emperor, . . . or to governors" (2:13–14). It is significant that the author specifically identifies the emperor (*basileus*) as well as local governors who would have been a visible presence of the authority of Caesar in Anatolia. This explicit identification accents Roman occupation and power for these Christians of various ethnicities. And Rome was not shy about emphasizing its might and "giftedness" to rule other peoples. We can discern this emphasis in Virgil's lines from the *Aeneid* (6.851–53)—this

49. Balch, *Let Wives Be Submissive*, 94. Areius Didymus (from his epitome of Aristotle's philosophy [first century BCE]) writes that sedition occurs "when those who are unequal have equality" (translation in Balch, "Household Codes," 43 [see 41n33]).

Roman poet's epic poem that would have been well known across the empire:[50]

> Tu regere imperio populos, Romane, memento
> (hae tibi erunt artes), pacisque imponere morem,
> parcere subiectis et debellare superbos.
>
> Do you remember, Roman, to rule imperially over the nations
> (these shall be your skills), to set the force of habit upon peace,
> to spare those who submit and crush in war the haughty.[51]

"To spare those who submit" points to the "ideal" good subject of the realm—one who is fully loyal to Rome. The common fate of all Rome's subjugated peoples, including the Petrine audience, was their required fealty to Rome and to Caesar. Given Rome's ultimate control and authority and Caesar's claims of lordship, how do these believers live out their allegiance to Jesus as the one true Lord? The rest of the paragraph suggests the way forward for them.

We should note that this command to submit is *unmarked*, which means that it fits expectations and does not press against genre boundaries. Yet the way the author frames the exhortation to submit already has a limiting effect on the scope of authority

50. For the significant influence of Virgil's *Aeneid*, see Longenecker, "Intertextuality in Pompeian Plaster," 31. Longenecker catalogs the seventy-nine citations of popular Greco-Roman works in the graffiti found in Pompeii and studies the thirty-six graffiti (almost half) that reference Virgil's *Aeneid*. He explores the significance of this preponderance and refers to the *Aeneid* as "in the air" in the pro-Roman town of Pompeii, with its use often functioning "to activate the pro-Roman sentiment of Virgil's text."

51. Text and translation from Horsfall, *Virgil, "Aeneid,"* 59 (although he sets this section in prose lines). David Horrell refers to the final line cited here to illustrate a Roman view of Roman strength and provides the translation, "to pardon those who submit and to subdue the proud" ("Between Conformity and Resistance," 127).

granted to the emperor and his delegates. By referencing the broad category as *anthrōpinē ktisei*, "human authority" or "human creature," the author has identified "the emperor and his representatives only as human creatures,"[52] and so "implicitly denies any claim that the emperor is θεῖος, 'divine.'"[53]

The command to submission is followed by a series of explanations and exhortations that illuminate the social pressures being experienced by his audience and that confound societal norms for "appropriate" political behavior. The author follows up the call to submission with an explanation that by doing so his audience might "silence the uninformed words of ignorant people" (2:15). This motif fits what I earlier described as the circumstances of the letter's recipients; they are experiencing verbal slander from neighbors, friends, even family members for their new loyalty to Christ.[54]

The *marked* features in this part of the household code come in the exhortations of 2:16–17. First, the author guides his readers to live out their submission in the *polis* "as those who are free" (*hōs eleutheroi* [2:16]). This is a striking identification for people living under Roman occupation, and it envisions a different possibility than simple acquiescence to Roman power. It empowers those with little political capital to reconceive their identity in line with God's salvific actions and perspective—a task the author has already begun to do in 2:4–10. Even as the author provides a potent vision for their identity as a free people, he qualifies that freedom: "not using your freedom as a guise for evil; instead, live as slaves of God" (2:16). We hear in this juxtaposition the pressures facing the Petrine audience to live out their new identity and allegiance to the one true God

52. Elliott, *1 Peter*, 489.

53. Horrell, "Between Conformity and Resistance," 135.

54. Although there is no explicit noun for "words" or "talk" (NIV) in the Greek, the use of the verb "silence" (*phimoō*) implies that the nature of the complaints against these Christians is being expressed verbally.

while avoiding, whenever possible, accusations of antisocial (i.e., anti-*polis*) behavior. As we have already noted, these accusations are already being leveled at them (4:3–4).[55] What is pronounced about this exhortation is that their identity as free people with respect to the state is guided by their identity as slaves with respect to God. And it is this divine relationship, not their relationship with Rome, that keeps their behavior in check. This is not something we would expect to hear in Plato or Aristotle or those who followed their lead.

A second marked feature of the code comes in 2:17, where the author provides four short and coordinating exhortations for relating to various others: "Honor all people, love the family of believers, fear God, honor the emperor." What stands out among these four exhortations for our purposes is the equalization of the first and fourth entities: "honor all people, . . . honor the emperor" (with *timaō* used in both cases). In this schema, the emperor is not granted a posture any greater than what is due to all people, and certainly not the fear and reverence (*phobos*) reserved for God alone.[56] In a context in which honor is given in decidedly differing amounts to different people and groups, this egalitarian stance

55. Travis Williams helpfully explores whether the good conduct that the author commends for his audience is socially compliant behavior (i.e., behavior that nonbelievers would recognize as "good" from their own vantage point) or is the very behavior that has been the impetus for the slander they are experiencing from nonbelievers stemming from their allegiance to Christ. He writes, "The good deeds in 1 Peter are not simply an appropriate *response* to the conflict situation; in many cases, they are one of the original *causes*. While doing good might occasionally result in a positive outcome such as the conversion of unbelievers (3.1), it normally produced adverse responses and therefore only further exacerbated the problems with outsiders (2.20; 3.14, 16, 17). For this reason, it does not seem adequate to describe this behaviour as conduct in conformity to socially acceptable norms—whether it is civic benefaction or any other form of social compliance" (*Persecution in 1 Peter*, 268–69). From a differing perspective, David Horrell suggests that "the author's notion of what is 'good' is evidently (taken to be) shared in common with those outside" ("Between Conformity and Resistance," 133).

56. Williams, *Persecution in 1 Peter*, 254; Horrell, "Between Conformity and Resistance," 135.

toward all people, including Caesar, is nothing short of astonishing, even if subtly expressed.[57]

### To Petrine Slaves: Relating to Their (Unbelieving) Master (2:18–25)

The household code moves to address slaves specifically in 2:18–25. We have already noted that in ancient domestic codes one would expect to hear the master-slave relationship discussed. Yet the conventional pattern in this genre is for guidance to be addressed to masters, not to slaves.[58] In the Petrine code, masters are not addressed at all, and household slaves (*oiketai* [2:18]) receive the longest discourse in the entire code (2:18–25).[59] This marked feature of the Petrine domestic code points to a greater sense of *agency* for these slaves, even in the difficult situations in which they find themselves.[60] As Shively Smith notes, "It is striking that 1 Peter does not address the master class at all."[61]

The admonition to slaves begins like this (2:18–19):

> Household slaves, submit in all fear to your masters, not only to masters who are good and tolerant but to masters who are perverse.

57. Williams suggests that it is "probable that 1 Pet. 2.13–17 represents a subtle critique of the emperor and his cult" (*Persecution in 1 Peter*, 253).

58. Balch notes a Jewish precedent for addressing slaves directly in Philo, *On the Special Laws* 2.67–68; 3.137; Testament of Joseph 10:1–3; 11:1–2 ("Household Codes," 46).

59. The term used, *oiketēs* ("household slave"), is more specific than *doulos* ("slave"), and the author may have used the former both to locate the issues being experienced squarely within the household and also to distinguish the relationship of slaves to their human masters from their relationship (as *doulos*) with their God just mentioned ("slaves of God," *theou douloi* [2:16]). Smith suggests the importance of the latter distinction, highlighting that Jesus as Lord and the Petrine community as "slaves of God" preempts any other master-slave relationship, including that of master (*despotēs*) and slave (*oiketēs*) in the household (2:18) (*Strangers to Family*, 74).

60. Joel Green comments, "Because in some circles in antiquity slaves were regarded as persons devoid of critical faculties, that Peter addresses slaves at all is significant; that he calls upon them to exercise discernment and moral agency in relation to the will of God is especially suggestive" (*1 Peter*, 80).

61. Smith, *Strangers to Family*, 72.

> For this is commendable: if, because of being conscious of God, someone endures pain, when suffering unjustly.

The situation of these slaves is intimated by the author's reference to submission even to masters (slave owners) who are "perverse" (*skolios*), not only to those who are good and/or "tolerant" (*epieikēs*).[62] By contrasting these two types of masters and by putting end emphasis on those who are "perverse" (i.e., not "tolerant"), the author focuses special attention on slaves whose masters are not allowing for dissent as it relates to loyalty to the family's gods.[63] This situation resonates with the admonition ahead to the Christian wives to submit to their husbands even if their husband is not a believer (and instead is "disobeying the gospel" [3:1]). These references suggest that at least some, if not many, of the Petrine households are divided in their allegiances, with those with significantly less power in the system struggling to live out allegiance to Christ, even as their *paterfamilias* remains committed to his gods and his past way of life.[64] As David Balch argues, "The author was especially concerned about divided households: many masters and husbands were still pagans while some slaves and wives had converted to Christianity. In these divided houses, the harmony demanded by the Hellenistic moralists had been disturbed, which was judged to be a negative reflection on the new religion."[65]

This situation would have put these women and slaves in a precarious position in the household. It is no wonder, then, that the

62. BDAG defines *epieikēs* as "not insisting on every right of letter of law or custom" and provides "yielding" and "tolerant" as two of its translation equivalents (371). Ceslas Spicq provides the following definition: "For those in positions of superiority, *epieikeia* is an easy-going quality that moderates the inflexible severity of wrath" (*TLNT*, 34).

63. John Elliott suggests that pagan masters are in view here (*1 Peter*, 516).

64. Smith, *Strangers to Family*, 71, 75.

65. Balch, *Let Wives Be Submissive*, 109; contra Horrell, who contends that the language suggests that "not all, or even most, of the wives in the Christian community were in this situation" ("Between Conformity and Resistance," 134n85).

author devotes the bulk of the domestic code to these two groups. And it would be no surprise that he presses the genre boundaries of his household code to affirm the agency of these two groups in their mission to stay loyal to Christ.

To these household slaves, the author calls for submission to their masters, as he has previously called his entire audience to submit to governing authorities (2:13 [with *hypotassō* at 2:13, 18; also 3:1]). As we noted there, this is an unmarked—that is, conventional and so unremarkable—feature of the code. Submission "in all fear" would often be the safest pathway for slaves in response to masters, who could assume and even enforce compliance in all things.[66] Certainly, unbelieving masters would expect adherence to their own religious allegiances from their slaves and would have no reason to be sympathetic to a slave's competing religious loyalties.[67] Given the way slaves, both male and female, and young and old, often were treated by their masters—treatment that could involve physical, sexual, and verbal abuse[68]—the author of 1 Peter provides active ways to combat what might be impossible situations. Specifically, he encourages slaves to "do good" and to endure even unjust suffering through their "awareness of God" (2:19–20). In these exhortations, the agency of these slaves is assumed and valued. As Smith proposes, "The letter maintains a judicious distinction between household servants and masters, portraying them as independent decision makers

66. While the phrase "in all fear" (*en panti phobō* [2:18]) likely refers to the posture of these slaves before God (cf. 1:17; 2:17), the author and audience undoubtedly would recognize in this language how easy it would be for slaves to fear for their safety under the authority of their masters.

67. Elliott writes, "As a general rule, slaves were obligated to the religion of their owners" (*1 Peter*, 516).

68. The Roman Stoic Musonius Rufus provides examples of injustice (*adikia*) by masters: "In this category belongs the man who has relations with his own slave-maid, a thing which some people consider quite without blame, since every master is held to have in his power to use his slave as he wishes" (12.30–34 [*That One Should Disdain Hardships*, 60]). For a helpful overview of vulnerability of slaves in households, see Osiek and MacDonald, *A Woman's Place*, 95–117.

within the traditional household. Just as the master can be gentle or harsh (1 Pet. 2:18), the servant can choose to do good or bad (1:19–20)."[69]

After giving these exhortations, the author provides slaves the example of Jesus, who suffered injustice yet did not deserve that treatment and was also innocent of retaliation. Jesus lived out the good in the midst of an impossible situation. Notice that it is not the slave owner who receives the words about Christ's example but rather slaves specifically who are invited to "follow in [Christ's] footsteps" (2:21).[70] This is a tricky interpretive and contextualizing moment in the letter since it can be all too easy to press those with least power in a system to imitate Jesus and sacrifice themselves without thought to issues of power and agency. Yet we should note that the vision of Jesus suffering injustice without returning violence could provide a keen sense of solidarity for the slaves of the Petrine churches. As Dennis Edwards notes, "Jesus is the one who is in solidarity with the sufferer."[71] We must also consider the very limited options of slaves in relation to masters, who would not have approved of their slave's newfound allegiance to Christ. Within their limited options, slaves, seeking to be above reproach in their behavior by living out the good without compromising their loyalty to Christ, could preserve their physical life. As Smith suggests, "Survival, not reprisal, appears to be the letter writer's priority."[72]

69. Smith, *Strangers to Family*, 73.

70. While the author likely wants the words of 2:21–25 to be appropriated by all believers (given its shared themes with other parts of the letter addressed to the entire community), it is important to acknowledge and grapple with the fact that Jesus' example is here explicitly given to slaves. Those with the hardest lot are connected most closely to Jesus' experience as a source of solidarity and encouragement.

71. Edwards, *1 Peter*, 124.

72. Smith, *Strangers to Family*, 74. Later, Smith sums up this strategy for the entire Petrine audience: "The author commands submission not because it was God's way but because it was his way of mitigating the conspicuousness of his community and keeping his members alive" (165). As Smith turns to reflect on her African American ancestors who were enslaved, she notes the role of "social

### To Petrine Wives: Relating to Their (Unbelieving) Husband (3:1–6)

The domestic codes turn from addressing house slaves to directly communicating with wives, and especially focusing on wives whose husbands are not part of the faith community—those who "are disobeying the word" (3:1).[73] The address begins and ends as follows (3:1–2, 6):

> Likewise, wives, submit yourselves to your own husbands, so that, if some of them are disobeying the word of good news, they might be won over by the wives' conduct without a word, by observing your reverent and holy conduct. . . .
>
> Sarah obeyed Abraham, calling him "lord." You become her children when you continue to do good and do not fear any intimidation.

What is eye-catching about this section is that wives are addressed directly and that they are addressed before husbands are, and at length (3:1–6), with a brief word to husbands coming in a single verse at the end of the domestic code (3:7). As we noted with the direct address to slaves, this feature suggests a greater amount of personal agency ascribed to those with less power in the household.[74] Caroline Johnson Hodge identifies the tension implicit in this passage when she writes that 3:1–6 "assumes a wife's agency precisely in her subservience."[75]

The address to wives begins, similarly to the previous two segments, with an exhortation to "submit" (*hypotassō* [2:13, 18;

---

compliance" of these slaves that allowed "their progeny [to] live to fight another day" (169).

73. The author's use of *logos* here is very likely a synonym for *euangelion* ("the gospel"), as at 1:23; 2:8; cf. 4:17, where the same verb for "disobey" (*apeitheō*) is used with *euangelion*. See Reese, *1 Peter*, 169–70.

74. Karen Jobes notes that the direct address, in each case, "implies that both [slaves and wives] have a measure of moral responsibility and choice unprecedented in Greek thought" (*1 Peter*, 204).

75. Johnson Hodge, "'Holy Wives,'" 3.

3:1]).[76] As in the other two cases, the call to submission is the expected feature of the household code, and so here is an unmarked feature of the address to wives. In other words, "The command for wives to submit to their unbelieving husbands would not have raised eyebrows in the first-century context."[77] Within 3:1, a marked feature is the stated purpose of the command to submit: "that [their husbands] might be won over." In a context in which the family head made the decisions for the household, even and especially related to the family's gods, the intention that a woman would be instrumental in her husband's conversion is surprising and unconventional. For example, the philosopher Plutarch (ca. 49–119 CE), in his essay *Advice to Bride and Groom*, exhorts, "A wife ought not to make friends of her own, but to enjoy her husband's friends in common with him. The gods are the first and most important friends. Wherefore it is becoming for a wife to worship and to know only the gods that her husband believes in, and to shut the front door tight upon all [strange] rituals and outlandish superstitions."[78]

It's worth pausing here to reflect on this contrast. Plutarch represents the commonplace view that a wife will fully align her loyalties—human and divine—with her husband's allegiances. Quite differently, the author of 1 Peter speaks of the end goal of submission as winning her husband over to her singular loyalty to Christ. As we read 1 Peter 3:1, we should be struck more by the countercultural mission expressed than by the submission exhorted. The latter is expected and would have blended into the background for the first audience. In bold relief, they would have

76. The use of the adverb *homoiōs* ("likewise") in 3:1 links the call to wives here with the call to slaves to submit in 2:18. It will reappear in 3:7, for the exhortation to husbands (though not a call to submission).

77. Brown, "Silent Wives," 401.

78. *Advice to Bride and Groom*, 19 (Babbitt, LCL). Hering affirms that Plutarch "envisions a stratified [marriage] relationship," with the man "characterised as the ruler, the woman as the obedient member" (*Colossian and Ephesian* Haustafeln, 253).

heard the missional vision as extraordinary.[79] The delicate nature of this mission—turning their husbands to Christ rather than returning to his gods—explains, I suggest, the wordless mission that the author commends: "they might be won over by the wives' conduct *without a word* [*logos*]" (3:1).[80]

Margaret MacDonald situates the dangerous position these women are in: "Living on the crossroads between the church and the world, women who were married to unbelievers were especially susceptible to scrutiny [from outsiders]. 1 Peter 3:1–6 gives us every reason to believe that these women were being treated with hostility by mates who may also have played a part in the slander of the community."[81]

The wordless mission of wives whose husbands are not believers sits in some amount of tension with the commendation to mission that will soon be given to the entire community to be "ready at every turn to give an answer to everyone who asks you for the reason [*logos*] for your common hope" (3:15). How do we make sense of this tension, or what Smith calls the author's "double vision," at this point?[82] As I suggest elsewhere, "In a cultural context where rejection of the gods of one's husband is socially unacceptable, silent rather than verbal witness is one way to minimize accusations against the gospel and the church, while remaining true to the purpose of winning the unbeliever."[83] The

79. This the clearest missional moment in the letter of 1 Peter up to this point (cf. 2:9).

80. There is a wordplay on *logos* here: the husband's disobedience to "the word [*logos*] of good news" is directly addressed by the wife's silent witness and mission accomplished "without a word [*logos*]." See Brown, "Silent Wives," 398.

81. MacDonald, *Early Christian Women*, 198. One textual clue that points in this direction is the joining of the verb "disobey" (*apeitheō*) with the noun "word/gospel" (*logos*) in 3:1—a combination that occurs also at 2:8 (cf. 4:17) to identify those slandering the believing community.

82. Smith, *Strangers to Family*, 77.

83. Brown, "Silent Wives," 402. MacDonald points out the evangelistic impact these women could also have had on their slaves and children within their households (as their primary sphere of influence) (*Early Christian Women*, 203).

author envisions Christian witness in both cases, but a different kind of witness for vulnerable members of his communities. The author of 1 Peter is recommending "prudence" as the course of action for these wives.[84]

The rest of the direct address to wives confirms this path of prudence as these women pursue their carefully enacted mission. These wives of husbands who are not yet followers of Jesus are to act in ways—through a focus on the qualities of submission and gentleness—that will most effectively win their husbands to Christ (3:2–5). In the final lines of the address to wives, we hear one possible ramification of these women staying true to Christ. The author draws on the example of "Sarah [who] obeyed Abraham, calling him lord," and then assures these women that they are Sarah's children if they "continue to do good and do not fear any intimidation" (3:6). The reference to calling one's husband "lord" (or "master" [*kyrios*]) evokes the power differential between wives and their husbands since the husband as *paterfamilias* could invoke his absolute authority whenever he wished.[85] This power differential explains the strong language that follows about not fearing "any intimidation"—a combination of the typical verb for "fear" (*phobeō*) with a more unusual and potent noun, *ptoēsis*, expressing intimidation or terror.[86] In the situation being addressed, the most likely source of such intimidation is a woman's unbelieving husband.[87] "Coercion to renounce their allegiance to Christ would be the intimidation most close at hand for wives who had recently turned away from their

84. MacDonald, *Early Christian Women*, 200. I have been particularly struck by this line from MacDonald's work: "Thinking about early church women has, perhaps above all, led me to be cautious about interpreting conventional behavior as inconsequential behavior" (248).

85. And it provides another point of tension with the exhortations to all believers in 3:13–17, which include "set apart Christ as [the only] Lord [*kyrios*]" in 3:15. For a discussion of this tension, see Michaels, *1 Peter*, 165.

86. BDAG, 895.

87. Ok, "Children of Sarah," 113.

husbands' religious commitments."[88] Yet they are exhorted *not to fear* their husbands, even if they could have had good reason to do so.[89]

### TO PETRINE HUSBANDS WHO ARE BELIEVERS (3:7)

The final turn of the domestic code briefly addresses husbands, and particularly any *patresfamilias* (heads of households) within the church family (3:7).

> Likewise, husbands, live with your wife in the awareness that she is the weaker of the two of you, assigning honor to her as a co-inheritor of the gift of life. Do this, so that your prayers might not be thwarted.

The inclusion of 3:7 indicates that there are heads of household in the Petrine (house) churches, even if it seems that the majority or at least a significant contingent of their members are from households with divided loyalties (2:18; 3:1). As Janette Ok suggests, "The . . . singular address to believing husbands in 3:7 strongly suggests that marriages between believers are the exception, not the rule. The brevity of 1 Peter's exhortation to husbands also reflects that the author's concern in 3:1–6 is not with wifely submission but conflictual relationships with their unbelieving husbands as a result of their obedience to Christ."[90]

The author exhorts these believing husbands to live with their wives with the recognition of the wife's weaker position in the family and society (as "the weaker of the two of you").[91] The

88. Brown, "Silent Wives," 400.

89. MacDonald notes that this exhortation is countercultural, since fearing one's husband was considered a proper stance. Instead, they are to fear God (1:17; 2:17) and not their husbands (*Early Christian Women*, 198).

90. Ok, "Children of Sarah," 113.

91. The use of *skeuos* ("instrument" or "vessel") places emphasis on the bodies (BDAG, 927) of the wife and husband and so likely focuses on the comparison that a

way they are to live out this awareness is by assigning their wife honor (*aponemontes timēn*) because she is an equal heir of the life that God has imparted in salvation. While calling husbands to honor their wives would have sounded in some ways unremarkable in that context,[92] the sense that a man was due greater honor than a woman (if their social status was otherwise equal) was also assumed.[93] In the first-century world, honor was a limited commodity and was distributed unequally along the social strata. We can hear the inequality of honor due between a man and his wife in Philo, who writes about gender differences and concludes that "woman is not equal in honour with man."[94] Similarly, Josephus declares, "The woman, says the Law, is in all things inferior to the man."[95] Ulpian, a Roman legal expert of the late second century CE, writes, "There is greater *dignitas* [acquired influence plus entitled respect] in the male sex."[96] These examples help us to hear that the exhortation for husbands to

---

wife is physically weaker than her husband, while also allowing for other entailments, including the (social) vulnerability that arises from being the physically weaker partner (cf. discussion on 3:6). For further discussion, see Jobes, *1 Peter*, 208–9. Musonius Rufus acknowledges that "man's constitution is stronger and women's weaker," so that lighter and heavier tasks are assigned to each, respectively (Musonius Rufus, 4.15–19 [Lutz, *Musonius Rufus*, 46–47]; see Hering, *Colossian and Ephesian* Haustafeln, 248–49).

92. Ruth Anne Reese notes, "It was not uncommon for the pagan moralists of Peter's day to assert that treating one's wife with honor was more likely to result in a harmonious marriage" (*1 Peter*, 183). Yet she also highlights how the notion that all people are equally worthy of honor, communicated at 2:17, is "a potentially radical concept" (146).

93. Gardner, *Women in Roman Law*, 67. Paul Achtemeier notes "the lower value in which [women] are held in non-Christian society" in the first-century world and contrasts this to the Petrine exhortation for husbands to "apportion honor" to their wives and other women in the household (*1 Peter*, 217).

94. Philo, *Questions and Answers on Genesis* 1.27 (Marcus, LCL).

95. *Against Apion* 2.199 (Thackeray, LCL). Josephus uses here the term *cheirōn* ("inferior"). This view contrasts with the Petrine acknowledgment of a woman's weaker status (physical and likely social) without suggesting general inferiority. For the argument that the author refers particularly to social vulnerability, see Keener, *1 Peter*, 245.

96. Cited in Gardner, *Women in Roman Law*, 67.

grant their wives honor is noteworthy (it is "marked" to some degree).

Within the Petrine domestic code, a husband is to share honor with his wife and is to esteem her as one who is equally the recipient of God's gift of salvation ("as a coinheritor of the gift of life"). The address to the husband concludes with the only direct warning within the entire domestic code. The author hinges divine attention to the prayers of these *patresfamilias* on obedience to the command that they honor their wives. Their prayers will be impeded if they neglect to honor and treat their wives as their equals in the faith. This is a serious warning: if a husband neglects to treat his wife with honor and as a coheir of salvation, his "prayers to God are hindered and so have no effect—God does not listen to them."[97]

### *The Framing of the Household Code*

This analysis of the household code of 1 Peter has illuminated various unmarked and thus unremarkable features as well as its marked or unusual characteristics. To conclude our exploration, we will address briefly the frame that the author provides for the domestic code in 2:11–12 and 3:8–12.

> Beloved, I exhort you as sojourners and exiles, to avoid from the desires of the present age, which are at war with your very lives. Make sure your conduct is honorable among the gentiles, so that, when they accuse you of doing what is wrong, they might see your good deeds and glorify God in the day of his visitation. (1 Pet. 2:11–12)

> Finally, all of you, be like-minded, sympathetic, loving, compassionate, and humble. Do not repay evil with evil or slander with slander, but instead give a blessing, since to this you were called, so that you might in turn inherit a blessing.

97. Achtemeier, *1 Peter*, 218.

"For whoever desires to love life and to see good days
must stop their tongue from evil and their lips from speaking deceit;
that one must turn from evil and do good, they must seek peace and pursue it.
For the eyes of the Lord are on the righteous,
and his ears are attentive to their prayer;
but the face of the Lord is set against those who do evil."
(1 Pet. 3:8–12, quoting Ps. 34:12–16a [LXX 33:13–17a])

Although there is much to be said about how the author of 1 Peter frames the household code, for our purposes we can notice the refrain of *avoiding evil* and *doing good*. This simple pairing sums up quite well the themes in the household code's framing. Staying the course to avoid evil behavior—including any kind of retribution for the slander the audience is enduring—and to pursue a good and righteous course of action provides an important lens for understanding the purposes of the Petrine code. As we have observed in the details of the code, these Christians are to remain above reproach by pursuing good and never responding in kind to the slander outsiders are leveling at the community of faith.

Yet, as we have also noted, the situation of the Petrine audience is complicated by their singular allegiance to Jesus Christ. The author has affirmed that there will be times when their behavior will look wrong, even evil, to those around them because of that singular loyalty—for example, when a woman does not worship the gods of her husband. We hear of this kind of catch-22 in the opening frame (2:12): "Make sure your conduct is honorable among the gentiles, so that, when they accuse you of doing what is wrong, they might see your good deeds and glorify God in the day of his visitation" (i.e., in the final day, when God makes all things right). Ensuring that their conduct is honorable—good and not evil—will not, it seems, keep these believers from being accused of wrongdoing in the present. There may very well be something in their behavior that will be offensive to the society in which they live.

This is especially true for those on the underside of power in the household and in the *polis*. The imbalance of power in their situations means that those in authority over them could view them as wrongdoers, even as these believers were rightly living out their newfound loyalty to Christ and Christ's ways. Their behavior was not going to satisfy everyone. As Travis Williams summarizes the message to the Petrine churches, they "were instructed to comply with the standards of popular society as a way of preserving the basic safety of the most at-risk readers; yet, in each case, social conformity was balanced by some form of resistance which cautiously challenged existing social structures and quietly asserted the insubordination of the author."[98] As he employs the household code, the author's message is this: "With the gospel and the glory of God at stake [1:25; 2:12], [these] believers should submit to human institutions whenever possible (2:13), so that their only 'offensive' behavior arises from their complete allegiance to Christ."[99]

## Hermeneutical Considerations

As we turn our attention to the hermeneutical dynamics of the household code within 1 Peter, we again will engage the bidirectionality of the embedded genre with its macrogenre (see chap. 1). To explore this mutual influence, we can pose two questions about the audience of this particular New Testament letter: *Who needs a household code? What kind of household code does the Petrine audience need?* The first question leads us to

98. Williams, *Good Works*, 277. Williams goes on to suggest, "The author's response constituted a form of subaltern accommodation" (277). And Smith contends that the author is interested in seeing his audience "survive the system despite the system" (*Strangers to Family*, 169).

99. Brown, "Silent Wives," 401.

explore how the author of 1 Peter uses the genre of household code, and the second helps us discern how that code is adapted for the author's specific purposes (i.e., the impact of the letter on the code).

### *The Household Code's Impact on the Letter*

We begin with the more obvious hermeneutical question about the ways that the household code impacts the letter of 1 Peter—the *Who needs a household code?* question. First, as we have explored in this chapter, the Petrine domestic code shines a spotlight on the divided allegiances within (many of) the households among the letter's audience.[100] Particularly in the guidance provided to slaves and to wives, we hear of this tension that needed to be addressed and navigated in prudent ways. Second, and closely related, the household code contributes to the paraenesis of 1 Peter as it signals that *the way believers live in their grounded daily existence matters for the gospel* (e.g., 3:1). Allegiance to Jesus and pursuit of what God desires (e.g., 2:15, 19–20) are to work their way into every corner of the life of faith.

Third, a key contribution of the household code to 1 Peter centers on the code's apologetic function. As noted above, the frame of the code (2:11–12; 3:8–12) suggests a goal of helping the Petrine community demonstrate through their behavior that they were not a threat to cultural expectations or to Roman authority. David Balch emphasizes that the code functions to ameliorate criticism from those outside the believing community: "Many of the Christians addressed by the author had rejected traditional religion (1:18b), and the author exhorted Christians in the kind of behavior that would silence the negative reactions which such

100. And the Petrine household code implies that it should not be surprising that the gospel could disorder a typical first-century household, putting flesh on Jesus' statement that he came to bring a sword that may even divide families (Matt. 10:34–36).

conversions generated (2:11–12, 15)."[101] Even if some of the letter's recipients would not have been able to quell all negative evaluations of their new allegiance and their resulting "antisocial" behavior (4:3–4), the household code guides these believers toward any possible points of compliance with cultural norms and with their expected societal roles.

Finally, the Petrine household code highlights a christological theme that serves as an example for the audience and most specifically for slaves who are in the difficult position of holding firm to their loyalty to Christ in the face of opposition from their master. The author provides an extended excursus on the unwarranted mistreatment and suffering of Jesus (2:21–25),[102] a description that contributes to this already prominent theme across the letter (1:11; 3:18; 4:1, 13; 5:1).

### *The Impact of 1 Peter on the Household Code*

The second question we can ask to help us reflect hermeneutically is, *What kind of household code does the Petrine audience need?* This question focuses on the impact of the letter as a whole on the household code, especially as the typical domestic form has been adapted in some significant ways for the author's purposes. In each segment of the household code, we have been able to see the ways the author has nuanced and adapted traditional genre contours. While household codes typically endeavored to promote compliance and stability, the Petrine code has been reshaped to help these various Anatolian Christians survive in what seem to be precarious situations, in which their allegiance to Jesus is causing them to be maligned and, in some cases, threatened.

101. Balch, *Let Wives Be Submissive*, 109.

102. A rationale for prescribed behaviors is frequently a part of household code material, even if such points tend to be fairly brief (e.g., Aristotle, *Politics* 1.5 [1260a 11–14]).

The marked features of the Petrine household code—the ones that would have stood out to its readers and hearers—include exhortations (1) for all believers to live as "free people" (while being slaves of God, not of the empire); (2) for slaves to exercise their moral agency in pursuit of good and honorable behavior; (3) for wives to stay true to their singular commitment to Christ and to win over their husbands even if they experience intimidation to return to his gods; and (4) for husbands to bestow honor on their wives as they acknowledge their status as coheirs of salvation.

These countercultural threads in the Petrine domestic code would have "cautiously challenged existing social structures."[103] There is a certain level of resistance offered in the code, which transgresses its typical parameters focused on promoting conformity. Scholars routinely address this phenomenon, often with language that tries to get at the tension implicit in a resistant household code. Some of the ways they describe the resulting stance toward culture promoted across 1 Peter include "soft difference" (Miroslav Volf),[104] "polite resistance" (David Horrell),[105] "holy nonconformity" (John Elliott),[106] and "surviv[ing] the system despite the system" (Shively Smith).[107]

However we describe this tension, it is important for interpreting 1 Peter, including the domestic code within it, to reckon with the context of its advice that the audience *circumspectly confront their social context*. The letter offers the strategy of a thoughtful leader toward his beleaguered congregations as they are living between a rock and a hard place. The goal of the household code, and the letter more broadly, is to help the believers navigate with

103. Williams, *Good Works*, 277.

104. Volf, "Soft Difference."

105. Horrell, "Between Conformity and Resistance," 143. He also speaks of 1 Peter encouraging a stance of "distance and resistance," even while promoting alignment with certain cultural norms (142).

106. Elliott, *1 Peter*, 597.

107. Smith, *Strangers to Family*, 169. She speaks of a result of this tension as the audience's "double consciousness" (167).

circumspection the fine line between their two realities: cultural norms and their newfound faith. The author guides them toward conformity to these cultural norms whenever possible and resistance when absolutely necessary so that they will remain true to Jesus Christ as the only true Lord.

# FIVE

# Conclusion

## *What Do Matryoshka Dolls and the New Testament Have in Common?*

Matryoshka dolls, also known as Russian nesting dolls, are beautiful and fascinating objects. They originated in Russia just before the turn of the twentieth century, in a context where Russian folk art was growing in popularity.[1] The first Russian matryoshka is attributed to lathe worker Vasily Zvyozdochkin and artist Sergey Malyutin (1899). It was an eight-piece doll depicting a peasant mother, with her seven children nested within.[2]

Matryoshki (the plural) quickly became popular not just in Russia but internationally.[3] People seemed captivated by them,

1. Along with a fascination in the Russian nobility for the peasantry and for village life (Ertl and Hibberd, *Russian Matryoshka*, 5). A possible influence for matryoshka is a nesting doll (depicting a monk) from Japan that appeared in Russia in the 1890s (8).

2. Ertl and Hibberd, *Russian Matryoshka*, 8.

3. Matryoshki were taken to the 1900 Paris Exposition and were well received and, afterward, sought after (Ertl and Hibberd, *Russian Matryoshka*, 10).

and for good reason. They contain in themselves the element of surprise. These dolls suggest, and even promise, that a single thing might contain more than that one thing. The largest, outermost matryoshka doll looks, on its surface, to be a solitary item. But take a closer look, and the singular thing contains multiple things.

This special feature of a matryoshka doll—its ability to contain, and even conceal, multiple other dolls—has made it a ripe analogy for all sorts of disciplines and fields of study. Through a simple search in an academic database, you can find this metaphor used in such disparate fields as cardiac medicine, microwave technology, computational design, oncological treatment, insect populations, citizen engagement, and, fittingly, the relationship between Russian Orthodoxy and Ukraine.

This is the analogy that comes to my mind as I round the corner and now provide a final summary of embedded genres in the writings of the New Testament.

## Summary of Embedded Genres in the New Testament

Any biblical book contains a number of genres embedded or nested within it. Even a compact book, such as Ruth, contains more than one embedded genre: blessings (1:8b–9a; 2:4, 12, 19, 20a; 3:10; 4:11–12, 14),[4] an oath (4:9–10), and a genealogy (4:18–22). Nested within the macrogenre of Ruth are these lovely generic twists and turns.[5]

In this book, I have analyzed three literary forms that nest within the macrogenres of three New Testament books: a poem

4. As identified by Kim, "Prayer in Ruth," 117–20. Kim comments on the role of (the genre of) blessings in Ruth: "Coming at significant junctures in the book of Ruth, the blessings provide commentary on the movement of the story and the actions of its major characters. Against the background of loss and despair that marks the story's beginning, they stand out in stark relief, painting a portrait of Yahweh as a God who providentially supports and sustains his own people" (120).

5. Whether the narrative macrogenre is conceived as historical narrative, novella, short story, folktale, or otherwise.

in Paul's Letter to the Philippians, riddles across the Gospel of Matthew, and a household code that sits at the center of 1 Peter.

The first, the Christ poem in Philippians 2:6–11, is a contested embedded genre. Some scholars do not read this section of the letter as anything other than epistolary prose, albeit of an elevated style. I have argued in chapter 2 that this section of text is indeed poetry and that the change of genre is significant. The text itself gives clues of this change and invites readers to shift their genre expectations as they move from 1:27–2:4 (or 2:5) to 2:6–11. In this shift, paraenesis moves to doxology—exhortation expands to embrace exaltation.

In chapter 3, we studied what I consider to be an underidentified embedded genre in the Gospels: the riddle. While scholars readily recognize many forms within the teachings of Jesus (such as parable and proverb), the riddle has been identified less frequently and has received sustained treatment only in the scholarship of Tom Thatcher.[6] Looking at Matthew specifically, I have argued that riddles are a regular occurrence in the evangelist's recounting of the story of Jesus. Matthew even narrates a "riddling session" set during Jesus' final days (Matt. 21:23–22:46). If Matthew's Jesus often engages in riddles, then interpreters ought to carefully consider this embedded genre for understanding both how Jesus teaches and how Jesus is portrayed.

The final embedded genre I have addressed—the household code in 1 Peter—has been recognized by virtually all Petrine scholars.[7] Yet it can be worthwhile to explore the hermeneutical significance of this household code, which accounts for a quarter of 1 Peter and sits in a place of prominence at the relative center

6. Thatcher, *Jesus the Riddler* (2006) and *Riddles of Jesus* (2000).

7. Virtually all contemporary commentators on 1 Peter recognize the importance of taking account of the embedded genre of household code as they read the letter. Wayne Grudem is an outlier, mentioning the possibility of the author's reliance on *Haustafeln* and in quick order dismissing it as a relevant category for interpretation (*1 Peter*, 43–44). He does not interact with David Balch's work and thesis, though it had been available (1981) well before the publication of Grudem's commentary (1988).

point of the letter. In chapter 4, I have considered why the author of 1 Peter might use a household code as a strategy for guiding the letter's recipients in their particular sociohistorical situation. And I proposed a reading of the Petrine household code that attends to how it conforms to the conventions of that genre and also bends expectations of the ancient household code for the purpose of offering a way forward for its beleaguered audience.

## Concluding Hermeneutical Observations

Through looking at these particular embedded genres in the New Testament, I have been able to explore a number of relevant hermeneutical issues. The first is simply the act and art of noticing, and noticing carefully, genres that operate within other genres. Like a matryoshka doll, on first glance it can be easy to see only a book's macrogenre. Through this study, I have become more attuned to and more interested in the embedded genres of the Bible. Being sensitive to changes in genre, to the often-subtle movement between macro- and microgenres, can bring forth rich hermeneutical insights. The particular hermeneutical gains explored in this book include an increased awareness of distinctive purposes of different genres and the bidirectional hermeneutical influence between the macrogenre of a whole biblical book and an embedded genre within it.

First, by taking a close look at the contours and the role of an embedded genre in a larger work, we can become more aware of the respective purposes of both genres and how these purposes interact. When an author changes genre, she or he also changes goals, even if ever so modestly. By using embedded genres, authors adapt or expand their purposes. We saw this in Paul's crescendo from exhortations to doxology—praise to God in Christ—in Philippians 2:6–11, even as he continues his exhortation by providing the example of Christ for shaping the Philippian believers (2:5).

His purposes expand to include the purposes of the poetic or hymnic genre he employs, even as the paraenetic goals of this part of his letter continue to linger.

Second, in each chapter we have examined the bidirectional influence of an embedded genre on its macrogenre—a hermeneutical insight drawn from rhetorical studies on genre.[8] We most often initially (and quite properly) focus interpretive attention on how an embedded genre shifts our understanding of what the genre of the larger work is doing. Being sensitive to bidirectional influence invites us to consider as well how the larger work and its genre could be impacting the embedded genre, providing at least some amount of reshaping of that embedded form. In the last chapter, we explored how a household code is embedded at the center of 1 Peter and in the process is reshaped in some key ways from its typical use as an instrument promoting conformity. In this reshaping, especially as it heightens agency for those with less institutional power in the household, the Petrine domestic code subtly subverts the forms of patriarchy and slavery that such codes typically were meant to uphold.

What I want to affirm at this concluding stage is the symbiotic relationship between an embedded genre and the larger work in which it is embedded. This affirmation in no way exhausts the subject; instead, it opens up new avenues for further exploration. As a result of this study, my own curiosity has been sparked to explore New Testament poetry more broadly and with more detailed focus on both Greco-Roman and Jewish poetic conventions. I have also been led to consider how my reading of the Gospels can more conscientiously attend to the many and diverse embedded genres in the teachings of Jesus and within the evangelists' narrative rhetoric.

My hope is that the hermeneutical analysis I have provided in this volume, whether the interpretive theory set out in chapter 1

8. Auken, "Genres inside Genres," 166.

or the particular examples explored in the other chapters, will stimulate interest, discussion, and debate. Ultimately, I hope I have encouraged all those interested in biblical studies to press more deeply into the significance of genre analysis generally and embedded genres specifically. In the process, I trust that new and generative insights on the meanings of biblical texts will flourish.

# BIBLIOGRAPHY

Abrahams, Roger D., and Alan Dundes. “Riddles.” In *Folklore and Folklife: An Introduction*, edited by Richard Dorson, 129–43. Chicago: University of Chicago Press, 1972.

Achtemeier, Paul J. *1 Peter: A Commentary on First Peter.* Edited by Eldon J. Epp. Hermeneia. Minneapolis: Fortress, 1996.

Alter, Robert. *The Art of Biblical Poetry*. New York: Basic Books, 2011.

Auken, Sune. “Contemporary Genre Studies: An Interdisciplinary Conversation with Johannine Scholarship.” In *The Gospel of John as Genre Mosaic*, edited by Kasper Bro Larsen, 47–66. Studia Aarhusiana Neotestamentica 3. Göttingen: Vandenhoeck & Ruprecht, 2015.

———. “Genres inside Genres: A Short Theory of Embedded Genre,” *Discourse and Writing/Rédactologie* 31 (2021): 163–78.

Bailey, James L. “Genre Analysis.” In *Hearing the New Testament: Strategies for Interpretation*, 2nd ed., edited by Joel B. Green, 140–65. Grand Rapids: Eerdmans, 2010.

Bailey, James L., and Lyle D. Vander Broek. *Literary Forms in the New Testament: A Handbook*. Louisville: Westminster John Knox, 1992.

Bakhtin, Mikhail. *Speech Genres and Other Late Essays*. Translated by Vern W. McGee. Edited by Caryl Emerson and Michael Holquist. Austin: University of Texas Press, 1986.

Balch, David L. “Household Codes.” In *Greco-Roman Literature and the New Testament: Selected Forms and Genres*, edited by David E. Aune, 25–50. Society of Biblical Literature Sources for Biblical Study 21. Atlanta: Scholars Press, 1988.

———. *Let Wives Be Submissive: The Domestic Code in I Peter*. Society of Biblical Literature Monograph Series 26. Atlanta: Scholars Press, 1981.

Barker, Kevin. "Two Sons and Three Traditions." *Journal of Biblical Theology* 3 (2020): 50–63.

Bauckham, Richard. *Jesus and the God of Israel: God Crucified and Other Studies on the New Testament's Christology of Divine Identity*. Grand Rapids: Eerdmans, 2008.

Becker, Eve-Marie. "The Reception of 'Mark' in the 1st and 2nd Centuries C.E. and Its Significance for Genre Studies." In *Mark and Matthew II: Comparative Readings; Reception, History, Cultural Hermeneutics, and Theology*, edited by Eve-Marie Becker and Anders Runesson, 15–36. Wissenschaftliche Untersuchungen zum Neuen Testament 304. Tübingen: Mohr Siebeck, 2013.

Berlin, Adele. *The Dynamics of Biblical Parallelism*. Bloomington: Indiana University Press, 1992.

Bird, Michael, and Nijay K. Gupta. *Philippians*. New Cambridge Bible Commentary. Cambridge: Cambridge University Press, 2020.

Bockmuehl, Markus. *The Epistle to the Philippians*. 4th ed. Black's New Testament Commentaries. London: A. & C. Black, 1997.

Booth, Wayne C. *The Rhetoric of Fiction*. 2nd ed. Chicago: University of Chicago Press, 1983.

Brown, Jeannine K. *The Disciples in Narrative Perspective: The Portrayal and Function of the Matthean Disciples*. Academia Biblica 9. Leiden: Brill, 2002.

———. *1 Peter*. New International Commentary on the New Testament. Grand Rapids: Eerdmans, forthcoming.

———. "Genre Criticism and the Bible." In *Words and the Word: Explorations in Biblical Interpretation and Literary Theory*, edited by David G. Firth and Jamie A. Grant, 110–50. Nottingham: Apollos, 2008.

———. "Just a Busybody? A Look at the Greco-Roman Topos of Meddling for Defining *allotriepiskopos* in 1 Peter 4:15." *Journal of Biblical Literature* 125 (2006): 549–68.

———. *Philippians: An Introduction and Commentary*. Tyndale New Testament Commentaries. Downers Grove, IL: InterVarsity, 2022.

———. "The Rhetoric of Hearing: The Use of the Isaianic Hearing Motif in Matt 11:2–16:20." In *Built upon the Rock: Studies in the Gospel of*

*Matthew*, edited by Daniel M. Gurtner and John Nolland, 248–69. Grand Rapids: Eerdmans, 2008.

———. *Scripture as Communication: Introducing Biblical Hermeneutics*. 2nd ed. Grand Rapids: Baker Academic, 2021.

———. "Silent Wives, Verbal Believers: Ethical and Hermeneutical Considerations in 1 Peter 3:1–6 and Its Context." *Word and World* 24 (2004): 395–403.

Brown, Jeannine K., and Kyle Roberts. *Matthew*. Two Horizons New Testament Commentary. Grand Rapids: Eerdmans, 2018.

Burge, Gary. "Commandment." In *Dictionary of Jesus and the Gospels*, edited by Joel B. Green, Jeannine K. Brown, and Nicholas Perrin, 149–52. 2nd ed. Downers Grove, IL: InterVarsity, 2013.

Burridge, Richard. *What Are the Gospels? A Comparison with Graeco-Roman Biography*. 2nd ed. Waco: Baylor University Press, 2018.

Caneday, Ardel B. "He Wrote in Parables and Riddles: Mark's Gospel as a Literary Reproduction of Jesus' Teaching Method." *Didaskalia* 10 (1999): 35–67.

Carter, Warren. *Matthew and the Margins: A Sociopolitical and Religious Reading*. Maryknoll, NY: Orbis Books, 2000.

Cohick, Lynn H. *Philippians*. Story of God Bible Commentary. Grand Rapids: Zondervan, 2013.

Crenshaw, James L. "Riddle." In *The Interpreter's Dictionary of the Bible: Supplementary Volume*, edited by Keith Crim, 749–50. Nashville: Abingdon, 1976.

Cunningham, David S., Don H. Compier, and James L. Boyce, "The Classical Rhetorical Tradition and Christian Theology." In *To Teach, to Delight, and to Move: Theological Education in a Post-Christian World*, edited by David S. Cunningham, 13–34. Eugene, OR: Cascade Books, 2004.

Davies, W. D., and Dale C. Allison. *A Critical and Exegetical Commentary on the Gospel According to Saint Matthew*. 3 vols. International Critical Commentary. Edinburgh: T&T Clark, 1988–1997.

deSilva, David. "Appeals to 'Logos,' 'Pathos,' and 'Ethos' in Galatians 5:1–12: An Investigation of Paul's 'Inventio.'" In *Paul and Ancient Rhetoric: Theory and Practice in the Hellenistic Context*, edited by Stanley E. Porter and Bryan R. Dyer, 245–64. New York: Cambridge University Press, 2016.

Devine, Jodi A. "Epistolary Revelations: Reading Letters in Nineteenth-Century British Novels." PhD diss., University of Delaware, 2007.

Dobbs-Allsopp, F. W. *On Biblical Poetry*. New York: Oxford University Press, 2015.

Dunn, James D. G. "Christ, Adam, and Preexistence." In *Where Christology Began: Essays on Philippians 2*, 74–83. Louisville: Westminster John Knox, 1998.

Eastman, Susan Grove. *Paul and the Person: Reframing Paul's Anthropology*. Grand Rapids: Eerdmans, 2017.

———. "Philippians 2:6–11: Incarnation as Mimetic Participation." *Journal for the Study of Paul and His Letters* 1 (2011): 1–22.

Edwards, Dennis R. *1 Peter*. Story of God Bible Commentary. Grand Rapids: Zondervan, 2017.

Elliott, John H. *1 Peter: A New Translation with Introduction and Commentary*. Anchor Yale Bible 37B. New Haven: Yale University Press, 2007.

Ertl, Rett, and Rick Hibberd. *The Art of the Russian Matryoshka*. Boulder, CO: Vernissage, 2003.

Fabricatore, Daniel J. *Form of God, Form of a Servant: An Examination of the Greek Noun* μορφή *in Philippians 2:6–7*. Lanham, MD: University Press of America, 2010.

Fee, Gordon D. *Paul's Letter to the Philippians*. New International Commentary on the New Testament. Grand Rapids: Eerdmans, 1995.

———. "Philippians 2:5–11: Hymn or Exalted Pauline Prose?" *Bulletin for Biblical Research* 2 (1992): 29–46.

Filson, Floyd V. "How Much of the New Testament Is Poetry?" *Journal of Biblical Literature* 67 (1948): 125–34.

Fowl, Stephen E. *Philippians*. Two Horizons New Testament Commentary. Grand Rapids: Eerdmans, 2005.

———. *The Story of Christ in the Ethics of Paul: An Analysis of the Function of the Hymnic Material in the Pauline Corpus*. Journal for the Study of the New Testament Supplement Series 36. Sheffield: JSOT Press, 1990.

France, R. T. *Matthew*. New International Commentary on the New Testament. Grand Rapids: Eerdmans, 2007.

Gaebelein, Frank E. "New Testament Poetry." *Bibliotheca Sacra* 129 (1972): 247–49.

Gardner, Jane F. *Women in Roman Law and Society*. Bloomington: Indiana University Press, 1986.

Garland, David E. *Reading Matthew: A Literary and Theological Commentary*. New York: Crossroad, 1993.

Goppelt, Leonhard. *A Commentary on I Peter*. Edited by Ferdinand Hahn. Translated and augmented by John E. Alsup. Grand Rapids: Eerdmans, 1993. Originally published as *Der Erste Pretrusbrief* Kritisch-exegetischer Kommentar über das Neue Testament 12/1. Göttingen: Vandenhoeck & Ruprecht, 1978.

Gorman, Michael J. "Paul and the Cruciform Way of God in Christ." *Journal of Moral Theology* 2 (2013): 64–83.

Green, Joel B. *1 Peter*. Two Horizons New Testament Commentary. Grand Rapids: Eerdmans, 2007.

Grudem, Wayne A. *1 Peter: An Introduction and Commentary*. Tyndale New Testament Commentaries. Downers Grove, IL: InterVarsity, 1988.

Gupta, Nijay K. *Tell Her Story: How Women Led, Taught, and Ministered in the Early Church*. Downers Grove, IL: IVP Academic, 2023.

Hagner, Donald A. *Matthew*. 2 vols. Word Biblical Commentary 33A, 33B. Dallas: Word, 1993–95.

Hansen, G. Walter. *The Letter to the Philippians*. Pillar New Testament Commentary. Grand Rapids: Eerdmans, 2009.

Hawthorne, Gerald F., and Ralph P. Martin. *Philippians*. Rev. ed. Word Biblical Commentary 43. Grand Rapids: Zondervan, 2004.

Heiser, Michael S. "Monotheism, Polytheism, Monolatry, or Henotheism? Toward an Assessment of Divine Plurality in the Hebrew Bible." *Bulletin for Biblical Research* 18 (2008): 1–30.

Heller, Barbara. Introduction to *Pride and Prejudice: The Complete Novel, with Nineteen Letters from the Characters' Correspondence, Written by Hand*, by Jane Austen, 6–12. San Francisco: Chronicle Books, 2020.

Hellerman, Joseph H. *Reconstructing Honor in Roman Philippi:* Carmen Christi *as* Cursus Pudorum. Society for New Testament Studies Monograph Series 132. Cambridge: Cambridge University Press, 2008.

Hering, James P. *The Colossian and Ephesian* Haustafeln *in Theological Context: An Analysis of Their Origins, Relationship, and Message*. American University Studies 7: Theology and Religion 260. New York: Peter Lang, 2007.

Hirsch, E. D., Jr. *Validity in Interpretation*. New Haven: Yale University Press, 1967.

Hirsch, Edward. *A Poet's Glossary*. New York: Houghton Mifflin Harcourt, 2014.

Horrell, David G. "Between Conformity and Resistance: Beyond the Balch-Elliott Debate towards a Postcolonial Reading of 1 Peter." In *Becoming Christian: Essays on 1 Peter and the Making of Christian Identity*, 211–38. Library of New Testament Studies 394. London: Bloomsbury T&T Clark, 2013.

Horsfall, Nicholas. *Virgil, "Aeneid" 6: A Commentary*. Vol. 1, *Introduction, Text and Translation*. Berlin: de Gruyter, 2013.

Jeremias, Joachim. *New Testament Theology: The Proclamation of Jesus*. New York: Charles Scribner's Sons, 1971.

———. "Zu Phil ii 7: ΕΑΥΤΟΝ ΕΚΕΝΩΣΕΝ." *Novum Testamentum* 6 (1963): 182–88.

Jobes, Karen H. *1 Peter.* Baker Exegetical Commentary on the New Testament. 2nd ed. Grand Rapids: Baker Academic, 2022.

Johnson Hodge, Caroline E. "'Holy Wives' in Roman Households: 1 Peter 3:1–6." *Journal of Interdisciplinary Feminist Thought* 4, no. 1 (Summer 2010): 1–24.

Jones, Ivor H. *The Matthean Parables: A Literary and Historical Commentary*. Supplements to Novum Testamentum 80. Leiden: Brill, 1995.

Keener, Craig S. *A Commentary on the Gospel of Matthew*. Grand Rapids: Eerdmans, 1999.

———. *1 Peter: A Commentary.* Grand Rapids: Baker Academic, 2021.

Keown, Mark J. *Philippians*. 2 vols. Evangelical Exegetical Commentary. Bellingham, WA: Lexham, 2017.

Kim, Brittany D. "Prayer in Ruth and Esther." In *Praying with Ancient Israel: Exploring the Theology of Prayer in the Old Testament*, edited by Phillip G. Camp and Tremper Longman III, 117–33. Abilene, TX: Abilene Christian University Press, 2015.

Klein, William W., Craig L. Blomberg, and Robert L. Hubbard Jr. *Introduction to Biblical Interpretation*. 3rd ed. Grand Rapids: Zondervan, 2017.

Köstenberger, Andreas J., and Richard D. Patterson. *Invitation to Biblical Interpretation: Exploring the Hermeneutical Triad of History, Literature, and Theology*. Grand Rapids: Kregel, 2011.

Langley, Wendell E. "The Parable of the Two Sons (Matthew 21:28–32) against Its Semitic and Rabbinic Backdrop." *Catholic Biblical Quarterly* 58 (1996): 228–43.

Larsen, Kasper Bro. "Introduction: The Gospel of John as Genre Mosaic." In *The Gospel of John as Genre Mosaic*, edited by Kasper Bro Larsen, 13–24. Studia Aarhusiana Neotestamentica 3. Göttingen: Vandenhoeck & Ruprecht, 2015.

Longenecker, Bruce W. "Intertextuality in Pompeian Plaster: Can Vesuvian Artifacts Inform Our Expectations about Intertextual Expertise among Early Jesus-Followers?" In *Practicing Intertextuality: Ancient Jewish and Greco-Roman Exegetical Techniques in the New Testament*, edited by Max J. Lee and B. J. Oropeza, 27–42. Eugene, OR: Cascade Books, 2021.

Longman, Tremper, III. *Literary Approaches to Biblical Interpretation*. Grand Rapids: Academie Books, 1987.

Lutz, Cora E. *Musonius Rufus: "The Roman Socrates."* Yale Classical Studies 10. New Haven: Yale University Press; London: Oxford University Press, 1947.

Luz, Ulrich, *Matthew 8–20: A Commentary*. Translated by James E. Crouch. Edited by Helmut Koester. Hermeneia. Minneapolis: Fortress, 2001.

———. *Matthew 21–28: A Commentary*. Translated by James E. Crouch. Edited by Helmut Koester. Hermeneia. Minneapolis: Fortress, 2005.

MacDonald, Margaret Y. *Early Christian Women and Pagan Opinion: The Power of the Hysterical Woman*. Cambridge: Cambridge University Press, 1996.

Mäntynen, Anne, and Susanna Shore. "What Is Meant by Hybridity? An Investigation of Hybridity and Related Terms in Genre Studies." *Text & Talk* 34, no. 6 (2014): 737–58.

Maranda, Elli Köngäs. "Theory and Practice of Riddle Analysis." *The Journal of American Folklore* 84, no. 331 (January–March 1971): 51–61.

Marshall, I. Howard. *New Testament Theology: Many Witnesses, One Gospel*. Downers Grove, IL: InterVarsity, 2004.

Martin, J. R., and David Rose. *Genre Relations: Mapping Culture*. London: Equinox, 2008.

Martin, Michael Wade, and Bryan A. Nash. "Philippians 2:6–11 as Subversive *Hymnos*: A Study in the Light of Ancient Rhetorical Theory." *Journal of Theological Studies* 66 (2015): 90–138.

Martin, Ralph P. Carmen Christi*: Philippians ii.5–11 in Recent Interpretation and in the Setting of Early Christian Worship*. Cambridge: Cambridge University Press, 1967.

Michaels, J. Ramsey. *1 Peter.* Word Biblical Commentary 49. Grand Rapids: Zondervan, 2018.

Minear, Paul S. "Singing and Suffering in Philippi." In *The Conversation Continues: Studies in Paul & John in Honor of J. Louis Martyn*, edited by Beverly R. Gaventa and Robert T. Fortna, 202–19. Nashville: Abingdon, 1990.

Mitch, Curtis, and Edward Sri. *The Gospel of Matthew*. Catholic Commentary on Ancient Scripture. Grand Rapids: Baker Academic, 2010.

Moule, C. F. D. "Further Reflections on Philippians 2:5–11." In *Apostolic History and the Gospel: Biblical and Historical Essays Presented to F. F. Bruce on His 60th Birthday*, edited by W. Ward Gasque and Ralph P. Martin, 264–76. Exeter: Paternoster, 1970.

Musonius Rufus. *That One Should Disdain Hardships: The Teachings of a Roman Stoic*, edited by Cora E. Lutz. New Haven: Yale University Press, 2020.

Najman, Hindy. "The Idea of Biblical Genre: From Discourse to Constellation." In *Prayer and Poetry in the Dead Sea Scrolls and Related Literature: Essays in Honor of Eileen Schuller on the Occasion of Her 65th Birthday*, edited by Jeremy Penner, Ken M. Penner, and Cecilia Wassen, 307–21. Studies on Texts of the Desert of Judah 98. Leiden: Brill, 2011.

Neyrey, Jerome H. *Honor and Shame in the Gospel of Matthew*. Louisville: Westminster John Knox, 1998.

Nolland, John. *The Gospel of Matthew*. New International Greek Testament Commentary. Grand Rapids: Eerdmans, 2005.

Novenson, Matthew V. *The Grammar of Messianism: An Ancient Jewish Political Idiom and Its Users*. Oxford: Oxford University Press, 2017.

Oakes, Peter. *Philippians: From People to Letter*. Society for New Testament Studies Monograph Series 110. Cambridge: Cambridge University Press, 2001.

Ok, Janette H. "You Have Become Children of Sarah: Reading 1 Peter 3:1–6 through the Intersectionality of Asian Immigrant Wives, Patriarchy, and Honorary Whiteness." In *Minoritized Women Reading Race and Ethnicity: Intersectional Approaches to Constructed Identity and Early Christian Texts*, edited by Mitzi J. Smith and Jin Young Choi, 111–29. Feminist Studies and Sacred Texts. Lanham, MD: Lexington Books, 2020.

Osiek, Carolyn, and Margaret Y. MacDonald. *A Woman's Place: House Churches in Earliest Christianity*. Minneapolis: Fortress, 2006.

Paauw, Glenn R. *Saving the Bible from Ourselves: Learning to Read and Live the Bible Well*. Downers Grove, IL: IVP Books, 2016.

Perrin, Nicholas. *Jesus the Priest*. Grand Rapids: Baker Academic, 2018.

Reese, Ruth Anne. *1 Peter*. New Cambridge Bible Commentary. Cambridge: Cambridge University Press, 2022.

Reeves, Rodney. *Matthew*. Story of God Bible Commentary. Grand Rapids: Zondervan, 2017.

Riesner, Rainer. *Jesus als Lehrer: Eine Untersuchung zum Ursprung der Evangelien-Überlieferung*. Wissenschaftliche Untersuchungen zum Neuen Testament 2/7. Tübingen: Mohr, 1981.

Schnackenburg, Rudolf. *The Gospel of Matthew*. Translated by Robert R. Barr. Grand Rapids: Eerdmans, 2002.

Senior, Donald. *The Gospel of Matthew*. Interpreting Biblical Texts. Nashville: Abingdon, 1997.

Silva, Moisés. *Philippians*. 2nd ed. Baker Exegetical Commentary on the New Testament. Grand Rapids: Baker Academic, 2005.

Smith, Shively T. J. *Strangers to Family: Diaspora and 1 Peter's Invention of God's Household*. Waco: Baylor University Press, 2016.

Stein, Robert H. *The Method and Message of Jesus' Teachings*. Rev. ed. Louisville: Westminster John Knox, 1994.

Strauss, Mark L. *Mark*. Zondervan Exegetical Commentary on the New Testament. Grand Rapids: Zondervan, 2014.

Thatcher, Tom. *Jesus the Riddler: The Power of Ambiguity in the Gospels*. Louisville: Westminster John Knox, 2006.

———. *The Riddles of Jesus in John: A Study in Tradition and Folklore*. Society of Biblical Literature Monograph Series 53. Atlanta: Society of Biblical Literature, 2000.

Turner, David L. *Matthew*. Baker Exegetical Commentary on the New Testament. Grand Rapids: Baker Academic, 2008.

Volf, Miroslav. "Soft Difference: Theological Reflections on the Relation between Church and Culture in 1 Peter." *Ex Auditu* 10 (1994): 15–30.

Whitlock, Matthew G. "Acts 1:15–26 and the Craft of New Testament Poetry." *Catholic Biblical Quarterly* 77 (2015): 87–106.

Williams, Travis B. *Good Works in 1 Peter: Negotiating Social Conflict and Christian Identity in the Greco-Roman World*. Wissenschaftliche Untersuchungen zum Neuen Testament 337. Tübingen: Mohr Siebeck, 2014.

———. *Persecution in 1 Peter: Differentiating and Contextualizing Early Christian Suffering*. Supplements to Novum Testamentum 145. Leiden: Brill, 2012.

Williams, Travis B., and David G. Horrell. *1 Peter*. 2 vols. International Critical Commentary. London: T&T Clark, 2023.

Winston, David. *The Wisdom of Solomon: A New Translation with Introduction and Commentary*. Anchor Bible 43. Garden City, NY: Doubleday, 1979.

Winter, Bruce W. *Roman Wives, Roman Widows: The Appearance of New Women and the Pauline Communities*. Grand Rapids: Eerdmans, 2003.

Winzenburg, Justin. *Ephesians and Empire: An Evaluation of the Epistle's Subversion of Roman Imperial Ideology*. Wissenschaftliche Untersuchungen zum Neuen Testament 2/573. Tübingen: Mohr Siebeck, 2022.

Witherington, Ben, III. *Jesus the Sage: The Pilgrimage of Wisdom*. Minneapolis: Fortress, 2000.

———. *Matthew*. Smyth & Helwys Bible Commentary. Macon, GA: Smyth & Helwys, 2006.

Wright, N. T. "Joy: Some New Testament Perspectives and Questions." In *Joy and Human Flourishing: Essays on Theology, Culture, and the Good Life*, edited by Miroslav Volf and Justin E. Crisp, 39–62. Minneapolis: Fortress, 2015.

Zogbo, Lynell, and Ernst R. Wendland. *Hebrew Poetry in the Bible: A Guide for Understanding and for Translating*. UBS Helps for Translators. New York: United Bible Societies, 2000.

# INDEX OF AUTHORS

# INDEX OF SCRIPTURE AND OTHER ANCIENT WRITINGS

### Wisdom



### Sirach



## New Testament

### Matthew

## Colossians



## Hebrews



## 1 Peter



# Old Testament Pseudepigrapha

## Testament of Joseph



# Mishnah

## Avot



# Greek Philosophers

## Aristotle

*Politics*



## Plato

*Laws*